Royal Insignia

NINETY-EIGHT READINGS
ON THE BELIEVER'S CREDENTIALS —
HUMILITY, BROKENNESS, NOTHINGNESS,
DESTITUTION, LOWLINESS, ETC.

Compiled by
Edwin & Lillian Harvey

BRITISH ADDRESS
Harvey Christian Publishers UK
P.O. Box 510, Cheadle
Stoke-on-Trent, ST10 2NQ
Tel./Fax (01538) 752291
E-mail: jjcook@mac.com

UNITED STATES ADDRESS
Harvey Christian Publishers, Inc.
3107 Hwy. 321, Hampton, TN 37658
Tel./Fax (423) 768-2297
E-mail: books@harveycp.com
http://www.harveycp.com

Contents

Foreword

For many years, the subject of humility greatly interested my good husband and I as we studied this virtue in Scripture and in biography. Together, we gathered much material, and, before my husband's death, we had already prepared part of this book, but it was not yet God's time for its publication. We still had many things to learn.

The laws of the Kingdom of God are unerring. Humility and lowliness of spirit are conditions which bring the mighty God very near and provide a platform upon which He can display His power. We have a God Who works silently and in secret. The big, noisy, self-advertising method that is popular with the world, is at variance with Him. Rather than share His glory, God removes Himself until humbled, stripped, and broken, man comes as a suppliant, dependent wholly upon Him.

Paul learned this lesson well when he said, "Always bearing about in our body the dying of the Lord Jesus, that the life also of Jesus might be made manifest in our mortal body. So then death worketh in us, but life in you" (2 Cor. 4:10, 11). That was the law of the Kingdom.

Another writer has put it this way: "Materially, death occurs when the soul forsakes the body; but, spiritually speaking, death works in us whenever we sacrifice the visible to the invisible. In that measure, we become more and more separated from earthly things and introduced to the heavenly realities."

We are deeply indebted to Trudy, Barry, and Edwin Tait, Joan Henry, and Edward Cook for their assistance in the preparation of this book. It would never have reached the press but for their sacrificial labors. Oh may God bless these truths to those who minister to others!

Lillian G. Harvey
July, 1992

The Royal Insignia

Let this mind be in you, which was also in Christ Jesus: Who . . . made himself of no reputation, and took upon him the form of a servant . . . humbled himself, and became obedient unto death (Phil. 2:5-8).

THE Good Book tells us in its opening pages how man, God's highest creation, fell by pride which has henceforth become the insignia of the kingdom of this world. Read any advert; listen to the media, and you will immediately recognize the insignia of the serpent. If this be true, then every born-again child of God ought to wear the insignia of Christ in His humility, meekness, and lowliness.

Christ's life in the Gospels was one of entire renunciation of His royal aspect; if He were to redeem mankind, then He must, as the last Adam, walk as God had intended our first parents to walk. If the first Adam climbed, the last Adam must descend. If man soars, Christ must come in lowliness.

Because man seeks the highest seat, He took the lowest.

Because man wishes to be as the gods, He became man, even a babe.

Because man desires costly dwellings, He had not where to lay His head and began His life in a manger.

Because man chooses elite suburbs, Christ chose Nazareth as His home.

Because man strives for wealth, He became poor.

Because man disdains his inferiors, He often chose the poor and outcasts as His friends.

Because man chooses men of renown to rule and govern the nations, He chose humble fishermen from Galilee to be His disciples. — Lillian Harvey.

7

The life and death of our Lord Jesus Christ are a standing rebuke to every form of pride to which men are liable:

Pride of ability: "I can of mine own self do nothing."

Pride of birth and rank: "Is not this the carpenter's son?"

Pride of bigotry: "Father, forgive them; they know not what they do!"

Pride of intellect: "As my Father hath taught me I speak these things."

Pride of learning: "How knoweth this man letters, having never learned?"

Pride of personal appearance: "He hath no form or comeliness."

Pride of reputation: "A friend of publicans and sinners!"

Pride of respectability: "Can any good thing come out of Nazareth?"

Pride of self-reliance: "He went down to Nazareth and was subject. . . ."

Pride of self-will: "I seek not mine own will but the will of Him that sent me."

Pride of success: "He was despised and rejected of men."

Pride of superiority: "I am among you as he that serveth."

Pride of wealth: "The Son of man hath not where to lay His head." —*Emmanuel* (Birkenhead, England).

It had been a small mastery for Him to have drawn out His legions into array, and flank them with His thunder; therefore He sent foolishness to confute wisdom, weakness to bind strength, despisedness to vanquish pride; and this is the great mystery of the Gospel, made good in Christ Himself, Who, as He testifies, came not to be ministered to but to minister; and must be fulfilled in all His ministers till His second coming. —Milton.

Thus saith the Lord, Let not the wise man glory in his wisdom, neither let the mighty man glory in his might, let not the rich man glory in his riches: But let him that glorieth glory in this, that he understandeth and knoweth me (Jer. 9:23,24).

The Infallible Proof

Behold, his soul which is lifted up is not upright in him: but the just shall live by his faith (Hab. 2:4).

THE great test of whether the holiness we profess to seek or to attain is truth and life will be whether it be manifest in the increasing humility it produces. In the creature, humility is the one thing needed to allow God's holiness to dwell in him and shine through him. In Jesus, the Holy One of God Who makes us holy, a divine humility was the secret of His life and His death and His exaltation; the one infallible test of our holiness will be the humility before God and man which marks us. Humility is the bloom and beauty of holiness.

The chief mark of counterfeit holiness is the lack of humility. Every seeker after holiness needs to be on his guard, lest unconsciously what was begun in the Spirit is perfected in the flesh, and pride creep in where its presence is least expected. — Andrew Murray.

There was a nun who was renowned for her great miracles. The Pope heard of it and sent his servant, Phillip, to report on her witness and work. Bespattered with mud and weary from the long journey, the Papal messenger finally reached his destination and was ushered into the presence of the famous nun. Putting his muddy boot up, he asked if she would help him with it. Disdainfully she refused such a humbling task. Phillip returned to the Pope, saying, "Sir, you need not concern yourself. There is no miracle because there is no humility."

An experienced servant of God, Dr. Owen, said that, while popularity is a snare that not a few are caught by, a more subtle and dangerous snare is to be "famed for holiness." The fame of being a godly man is as great a snare as the fame of being learned or eloquent. It is even possible to attend with scrupulous anxiety to secret habits of devotion in order to get a name for holiness.

Archbishop Fénelon who tutored the son of King Louis XIV of France was an able and saintly man who valued highly humility, that Christian trait, admired on earth and honored in Heaven. "He who is conscious," he said, "that he is lowering himself has not yet reached his true place, which is below all lowering. Such as these are very proud in their humility, which, indeed, is often but a subtle spirit of vain glory. And this is not the humility which will enter into Heaven, unless it acquires pure charity, which alone is worthy of God, and which He delights to fill with Himself.

"They who are really thus filled never feel either humbled or lowered, for they count themselves as below all humiliation. Before they could humble themselves, they must rise from whence they are, and they would not leave that place to which God has called them. They are not humbled by men's contempt or condemnation, neither do they triumph in any applause, for neither concerns them. They think that One only, in taking upon Him the nature of man, humbled Himself."

> I want the first approach to feel
> Of pride, or fond desire;
> To catch the wand'ring of my will,
> And quench the kindling fire.
> —Charles Wesley.

When Dr. Cairns was Head of the Theological College in Edinburgh, he was offered the principalship of the university there, but declined it, preferring to serve his church in a humbler way. On public occasions, he was accustomed to stand back and let others pass him, saying, "You first, I follow."

When he was dying he said farewell to those whom he loved, but his lips continued still to move. They bent to catch the final word, which doubtless was spoken to Him Who was dearer to him than life—"You first, I follow." Such lowliness is one of the richest ingredients of love, and in its presence pride becomes an impertinence and an offence. —Graham Scroggie.

10

Unwelcome Demolition

Except the Lord build the house, they labour in vain that build it (Psa. 127:1).

AND they said, Go to, let us build us a city and a tower, whose top may reach unto heaven; and let us make us a name. . . ." These outspoken, misguided men voiced the intent of every human being who has lived since Adam. Since the fall, every man desires to build a tower and a name. The dominant child goes about it in the family. The growing boy does it on the field of sport. The young girl goes about it in the ballroom, or on the dance floor. In the school room, in the office, and alas in the church, we all want to build something.

We build egos, reputations, circles of influence, personal friendships, business empires, and so it goes—build, build, build. Our youthful energies, our budding intellect, and if we are not careful, our religious experiences, all go to build something. At its height, it takes expression in the words of the old king, Nebuchadnezzar, "Is not this great Babylon that I have built . . . ?"

The Psalmist David saw the folly of it all and exclaimed, "Except the Lord build the house, they labour in vain that build it."

God is the Universal Demolisher. He must destroy the fruits of our labors while there is time to build something that lasts. Jesus said that the man who built without His instructions was building on the sand. In love, our God would lay low our treasured castles of self, only that He might build.

His word to Jeremiah, newly commissioned as His prophet, was "to root out, to pull down, and to destroy, and to throw down." Only after these four operations of demolition were performed, could he proceed with God's help to build and plant (Jer. 1:10). Jesus said, "Every plant, which my heavenly Father hath not planted, shall be rooted up."

11

In our own day, we have all witnessed, sometimes with relief and sometimes with sadness, the ruthless process of demolition. A bulldozer can tear down in a few minutes the work of many months, performed so laboriously by hand a hundred or more years ago.

What concerns us here is, what is God doing with us? The self-righteous sinner, in a thorough repentance, finds his good-works' edifice tumbling around his ears. The "seventh of Romans" would-be saint finds his every self-effort at personal holiness worse than useless.

But do we recognize that in our Christian living and service we are in danger constantly of building in vain? And God in His great love tears down our little empires. We are crushed with disappointment and disillusionment.

Oh, to recognize the demolition of love! God strips David of Saul's armor that he might slay the giant "in the Name of the Lord" with a sling and a stone. This same God decimated Gideon's army from 32,000 to 300, or we might coin a word and say He "centimated" it, divided it by 100 rather than by ten.

The pulling down of precious things in our lives and in our little "empires" is unpleasant business. But our loving Father knows best. Let us hand the job over to Him and He will build that which will endure when this world is wrapped in flames. Then, in the words of Samuel Rutherford, we will "praise God for the hammer, the file, and the furnace." —E. F. Harvey.

> If God build not the house, and lay
>   The groundwork sure—whoever build,
> It cannot stand one stormy day.
> If God be not the city's Shield,
>   If He be not their bars and wall,
> In vain is watch-tower, men, and all.
> —Unknown.

The Frightful Ruins

Take away her battlements; for they are not the Lord's (Jer. 5:10).

MADAM Guyon, a devout, French Catholic woman of noble birth, attained great spiritual wisdom, through many revelations from the Holy Spirit. Her light was far in advance of most of her contemporaries, and God was enabled to use her mightily in the salvation of nuns, priests, and even much higher dignitaries within the Roman Catholic Church. For this she suffered banishment again and again, was denounced by her own church, and finally imprisoned within the Bastille. When asked to write her autobiography, she placed foremost in the book the most important truth she had gleaned throughout her varied history. She has left us these classic words:

"You will not attain sanctification save by much trouble and labor, and by a road which will appear to you quite contrary to your expectation. You will not, however, be surprised at it if you are convinced that God does not establish His great works except upon 'the nothing.' It seems that He destroys in order to build. He does it so in order that this temple He destines for Himself, built even with much pomp and majesty, but built nonetheless by the hand of man, should be previously so destroyed, that there remains not one stone upon another.

"It is these frightful ruins which will be used by the Holy Spirit to construct a temple which will not be built by the hand of men, but by His power alone. God chooses for carrying out His works either converted sinners whose past iniquity serves as counterpoise to the exaltation, or else persons in whom He destroys and overthrows that 'own' righteousness, and that temple built by the hand of men, so built upon quicksand, which is the resting on the created, and in these same works, in place of being founded on the living stone, Jesus Christ. All that He has come to establish, by entering the world, is effected by the overthrow and destruction of the same thing He wished to build. He established His Church in a manner that seemed to destroy it. Oh, if men knew how opposed is the 'own' righteousness to the designs of God, we should have an eternal subject of humiliation and distrust of what at present constitutes our sole support."

My bleak flagpole was stripped bare until my Master ran His colors up. — Rachel Rice.

Failure, the breaking down of men's confidences, the going to pieces of men's plans — failure means many things. One of the things which it means is this: that God will not let the soul hide behind any protection which He knows is insecure. His whole love binds Him to let the soul know its blunder before it is too late. . . . If you have known any such experience as that, you have been taken into one of the richest rooms of God's schoolhouse, one of the rooms in which He makes His ripest and completest scholars. Oh, if our souls today could mount to the height of some such prayer as this: "Lord, if I am building around the prosperity of my life any battlements which are not Thine, any defences of deceit or injustice or selfishness, break down those battlements whatever pain it brings, however it may seem to leave my hopes exposed." — Phillips Brooks.

Charles Spurgeon, the preacher who constantly depended upon the prayers of his people, always had a full house to which to preach. The secret of his usefulness might be discovered in his own words: "It seems that Jehovah's way is to lower those whom He means to raise and to strip those whom He intends to clothe. If it is His way, it is the wisest and best way. If I am now enduring the bringing low, I may well rejoice, because I see in it the preface to the lifting up. The more we are humbled by grace, the more we shall be exalted in glory. That impoverishment which will be overruled for our enrichment is to be welcomed.

"Oh, Lord, Thou hast taken me down of late, and made me feel my insignificance and sin. It is not a pleasant experience, but I pray Thee make it a profitable one to me. Oh, that Thou wouldst thus fit me to bear a greater weight of delight and of usefulness, and when I am ready for it, then grant it to me, for Christ's sake! Amen."

Pulling Down the Edifice

The weapons of our warfare are not carnal, but mighty through God to the pulling down of strong holds; Casting down . . . every high thing that exalteth itself against the knowledge of God (2 Cor. 10:4,5).

IT is astonishing how the same truth can become the property of Christians living over a century apart. The very truth which Madam Guyon, a French Roman Catholic, brought to our attention in the previous reading, was revealed to George Bowen, an American Presbyterian, many years later. Surely the same Holy Spirit was their common Teacher. We quote from Bowen's book, *Love Revealed:*

"Alas for those who are rearing up on high, storey above storey, a towering monument, intending, when it is done, to put the living Stone somewhere at the top, and so get the whole transported to Heaven! No, it must all come down, every stone of it; and it is to be feared that there will not be time for you to get it down and a new foundation laid before the great earthquake flies rumbling through the earth, for the cement that you are using hardens rapidly, and the stones cling together as though they naturally belong together; and you are bestowing so much ornament and there are so many admirers that you are every day more and more fascinated with your own work. Day by day you become more and more intensely your own ideal; and the demolition of a structure so laboriously reared, so expensively, seems to your conception like the crash of an expiring world.

"Then the schools of the world, so far from fitting their pupils for the school of Christ, make it less and less possible that those pupils should ever be brought to Christ. And here we discover a very important cause of the misunderstanding between the scholars of Christ and other scholars."

In another portion of his book, the author asks why it is that Christians should be hated by the world, when they are loving in disposition and always desirous of their fellowman's redemption. He then proceeds to answer his own question:

"Consider this: the mission of Christians is to take from men something that is unutterably dear to them, to reduce them to a condition that seems to them worse than slavery, to carry them away into perpetual exile, to foil them in every enterprise that they have at heart, in fact—we may as well say it—to kill them. Do you start back in horror? Hear me to the end.

"There is not anything so dear to the man of this world as the idea of his own unblamableness. Every day of his life he has been engaged in rearing, in his inner thought-world, a lofty edifice—a tower of Babel—to answer at once the purpose of a monument in his own praise, and to enable him, when the time shall come, to step from its pinnacle into Heaven. Every day he has been busy carving to some answerable shape the stones of his daily experience. He has diligently, all his life long, done battle with the insolent voices of a miscreant conscience, establishing by successive victories the difficult fact that he is, take him for all in all, one whom God must look down upon with benignity, if not with admiration.

"You come to him in the name of Christ for the very purpose of depriving him of this idea of his own goodness. Your aim is to do what that tormenting conscience of his, with all its advantages of time and place, failed to do. Do you think that he has fought with the Goliath of his own conscience so many times, and so successfully, to be now discomfited by you? Will he allow you to be victorious over him and take from him the idea of his own integrity in the sight of God, after he has gone through a thousand fights to obtain that pearl of price?

"You tell him that he is a mere rebel against the most high God, that he has never been anything else, that all his righteousnesses are contemptible in the sight of Heaven, that he deserves the wrath of God, and you ask him to take this same view of himself. You ask him to adjudge himself to be worthy of everlasting punishment. How easy were it for him in comparison to surrender all his worldly substance! Self-esteem permeates his whole nature like the fibers of a cancer, and to bid him part with it is like bidding him surrender life."

His Building Site — Our Ruins

O Israel, thou hast destroyed thyself; but in me is thine help (Hosea 13:9).
Gather up the fragments that remain, that nothing be lost (John 6:12).

HAROLD St. John was a profound Bible student who shared his riches with countless others. His daughter, Patricia, was a missionary for some years in North Africa. Out of the wealth of her experiences, she has written books for children which are on the market today. It is evident from her poem, that she had come to realize this secret of the Lord — that our failures and frustrations are the ruins which the Master Builder chooses for His site:

"My Master has an elixir that turns
All base and worthless substances to gold.
From rubble stones He fashions palaces
Most beautiful and stately to behold.
He garners with a craftsman's skilful care
All that we break, and weeping cast away.
His eyes see uncut opals in the rock
And shapely vessels in our trampled clay.
The sum of life's lost opportunities,
The broken friendships, and the wasted years,
These are His raw materials; His hands
Rest on the fragments, weld them with His tears.

"A patient Alchemist! — He bides His time,
Broods while the South winds breathe, the North winds blow,
And weary self, at enmity with self,
Works out its own destruction, bitter slow.
Then when our dreams have dwindled into smoke,
Our gallant highways petered out in mire,
Our airy castles crumbled into dust,
Leaving us stripped of all save fierce desire,
He comes, with feet deliberate and slow,
Who counts a contrite heart His sacrifice.

"(No other bidders rise to stake their claims
He only on our ruins sets a price).
And stooping very low engraves with care
His Name, indelible, upon our dust;
And from the ashes of our self-despair
Kindles a flame of hope and humble trust.
He seeks no second site on which to build,
But on the old foundation, stone by stone,
Cementing sad experience with grace,
Fashions a stronger temple of His own."

— Used by permission.

We found this lovely story in an old *Christian Herald:* "A poor apprentice once made a cathedral window out of discarded pieces of glass, which his master had thrown away. But when completed, the window won the admiration of all. The master's boasted work was rejected, and the window made from the condemned material was given the place of honor in the Cathedral. The wisdom of the world made its painted window of the wise, the learned, and the righteous, but the unknown Jesus of Nazareth became the Architect of a new society. He rejected the noble and the wise and chose the very material that the wisdom of the world had condemned, and from the refuse of society He has taken up fallen sons of men and set them, as gems, to sparkle forever in the diadem of His glory." — Mrs. G.

John Milne had offered himself as a candidate to the Missionary Society. And they, sorely in need of someone to send to assist Robert Morrison, were loathe to send him because of his many deficiencies. After highlighting his drawbacks, they offered him a post as servant rather than a missionary. John Milne replied: "If I am not judged fit to be a missionary, I will gladly go as a servant. I am willing to be a hewer of wood or a drawer of water, or to do any service that will advance the kingdom of my heavenly Master."

Years afterward, Dr. Milne was recognized by all men as one of the best and most competent workers in the land. God had taken up the fragments and built them into His missionary edifice in China.

Break My Primitive Tower

Let us build a city and a tower, whose top may reach unto heaven (Gen. 11:4).

A BLIND, Scottish minister, George Matheson, composed that beautiful hymn, "O Love That Wilt Not Let Me Go." If he had penned no other gem than this, he would have left posterity enriched; nevertheless, he also wrote numerous inspirational books which reveal the fact that he saw more deeply into the Scriptures than did many of his contemporaries. The truths which Madam Guyon and George Bowen have just shared with us, he has endorsed in his own unusual style. Commenting on the building of the tower of Babel, he shows how universal is man's ambition to climb:

"This world is a place where human beings are taught to climb, but it is to climb down. It is quite natural for us to go up. The writer of the Book of Job says, 'Man is born to trouble as the sparks fly upward.' I think he must have meant, 'Man is born to fly upward like the sparks, and therefore he is troubled.' At all events, that is true.

"Our early dangers come from our early daringness — not from our early feebleness. Young Adam always begins with the biggest tree and always gets a fall. God's education of the earth is a series of lessons in 'how to descend' in the moderation of desire. Christian prayer itself is a moderation of desire. It is a refusal any longer to say of everything, 'It is mine.' It is the refusal to ask that which will lift me above other people. It is the cry to have my garments parted among the multitude. It is the impulse, the determination, the instinct, to share.

"Lord, break my primitive tower! It is built with a child's arrogance, not with a man's humility; break my primitive tower! My feeblest moments are my most grasping moments — I am never such an egotist as in the cradle; break my primitive tower! Like the sparks I have been born to fly upwards, and to leave my brother behind. I need a second birth — a power to fly downwards. I need more weight on the wings; every weight will be to me 'a weight of glory. . . .'

"Lord, Thou hast arrested me on my Damascus journey. Thou hast transformed self-consciousness into humility. I set out on the road with boundless belief in myself; I felt no obstacle; I experienced no difficulty. Suddenly, at the turning of the way, my soul grew paralyzed. The confidence faded. The world no longer stretched before me as a pleasure-ground. There came a mist over the scene, and I could not find my way. It all happened in the meeting with one Man — a Man from Nazareth. Before I met Him, my pride of self was unbounded; I said in my heart, 'I shall carve my own destiny.' But one glance at the Man of Nazareth laid me low. My fancied glory became ashes; my imagined strength became weakness; I beat upon my breast and cried, 'Unclean!'

"Shall I repine because I met that Man? Shall I weep because a flash of light at a street corner threw all my greatness into shade? No, my Father, for the shade is the reflex of the sheen. It is because I have seen Thy beauty that humanity has grown dim. It is enlargement that has made me humble. I have gazed for a moment on a perfect ideal, and its brightness has eclipsed my candle. It is not night, but day, that blinds me to my own possessions. It is light that makes me loathe myself." — *Thoughts from Life's Journey.*

> Half feeling our own weakness,
> We place our hands in Thine —
> Knowing but half our darkness,
> We ask for light divine.
> Then, when Thy strong arm holds us,
> Our weakness most we feel,
> And Thy love and light around us
> Our darkness must reveal.
> — Unknown.

Humility by Aspiration

Lord, what is man, that thou takest knowledge of him! or the son of man, that thou makest account of him! (Psa. 144:3).

PHILLIPS Brooks was a much loved Episcopalian minister in Boston. His meditations on the Scriptures make for beneficial reading: "When Christ showed us God, then man had only to stand at his highest and look up to the Infinite above him to see how small he was. And always, the true way to be humble is not to stoop till you are smaller than yourself, but to stand at your real height against some higher nature that shall show you what the real smallness of your greatest greatness is. . . .

"Unreal humility always goes about depreciating human nature. Genuine humility always stands in love and adoration, glorifying God.

"Humility comes by aspiration. If, in all Christian history, it has been the souls which most looked up that were the humblest souls; if today the rescue of a soul from foolish pride must be not by a depreciation of present attainment but by opening more and more the vastness of the future possibility; if the Christian man keeps his soul full of the sense of littleness, even in all his hardest work for Christ, not by denying his own stature, but by standing up at his full height, and then looking up in love and awe and seeing God tower into infinitude above him—certainly all this stamps the morality which is wrought out within the idea of Jesus with this singular excellence, that it has solved the problem of faithfulness and pride, and made possible humility by aspiration."

There are two humilities, that which bows and that which soars, the humility of a servant who looks down, the humility of a son who gazes up. This latter makes religion not stiff and heavy with ceremonial, but simple, glad, and pleasing to God. —Professor Dowden.

Not wishful for a foremost place,
 Authority or power,
But just to gaze upon Thy face
 Daily and hour by hour.

Marking the lowliness that led
 Thy footsteps to the Cross,
The pain that Thou didst choose instead
 And utter earthly loss.

Shall I be proud of gifts that make
 My life more full and free?
Can I be vain when I but take
 Each benefit from Thee?

Down to the dust my soul sinks low
 At all the thankless pride,
That threatens as a deadly foe
 To tear me from Thy side.

Raise Thou me up, but not to power
 Not to a foremost place,
But till I learn each day, each hour,
 To gaze upon Thy face.
     —G. M.

I shall find it easy to humble myself when I compare my character with that of God, and I shall find it easy to take a low seat when I know my true condition. —Anon.

How lovely to think that when folk humble themselves God is not unmindful. You see, the eyes of the Lord are constantly on the humble people—He can't resist the humble person. The eyes of the Lord run to and fro throughout all the earth to show himself strong on behalf of those who fear him. The person who fears the Lord is a person who is humble, for to fear the Lord is to have an acute awareness of His presence. When you are aware of the presence of God, I'll tell you what, you're very small. We become big in our own estimation when we lose the sense of the divine touch on our lives, when we think that He has become a God afar off, that He's suddenly become remote. The true fear of God is a recognition of the immediate presence of God. And no one can be proud when aware of the presence of God. —Robert Cox.

The God-Blinded Soul

For I determined not to know any thing among you, save Jesus Christ, and him crucified. . . . that your faith should not stand in the wisdom of men (1 Cor. 2:2,5).

THOMAS Kelly was Professor of both Eastern and Western Philosophy in various Quaker colleges and secular universities throughout the United States. He came into a living, vital relationship with God at forty-four years of age which changed his entire outlook for the four brief years remaining to him. We quote from his deeply devotional book, *A Testament of Devotion:*

"What trinkets we have sought after in life, the pursuit of what petty trifles has wasted our years as we have ministered to the enhancement of our own little selves! And what needless anguishes we have suffered because *our* little selves were defeated, were not flattered, were not cozened and petted! But the blinding God blots out this self and gives humility and true selfhood as wholly full of Him. For as He gives obedience so He graciously gives to us what measure of humility we will accept. Even that is not our own, but His Who also gives us obedience.

"But the humility of the God-blinded soul endures only so long as we look steadily at the Sun. Growth in humility is a measure of our growth in the habit of the Godward-directed mind. And he only is near to God who is exceedingly humble. The last depths of holy and voluntary poverty are not in financial poverty, important as that is: they are in poverty of spirit, in meekness and lowliness of soul. . . .

"The fruits of holy obedience are many, but two are so closely linked together that they can scarcely be treated separately. They are the passion for personal holiness and the sense of utter humility. God inflames the soul with a craving for absolute purity. But He, in His glorious otherness, empties us of ourselves in order that He may become all.

"Humility does not rest, in final count, upon bafflement and discouragement and self-disgust at our shabby lives, a brow-beaten, dog-slinking attitude. It rests upon the disclosure of the consummate wonder of God, upon finding that only God counts, that all our own self-originated intensions are works of straw. And so in lowly humility we must stick close to the Root and count our own powers as nothing except as they are enslaved in His power.

"But O, how slick and weasel-like is self-pride! Our learnedness creeps into our sermons with a clever quotation which adds nothing to God's glory but a bit to our own. Our cleverness in business competition earns as much self-flattery as does the possession of the money itself. . . . Our status as 'weighty Friends' gives us secret pleasures which we scarcely own to ourselves, yet thrive upon. Yes, even pride in our own humility is one of the devil's own tricks.

"But humility rests upon a holy blindedness, like the blindedness of him who looks steadily into the sun. For wherever he turns his eyes on earth, there he sees only the sun. The God-blinded soul sees naught of self, naught of personal degradation or of personal eminence, but only the Holy Will working impersonally through him, through others, as one objective Life and Power."

> Worldlings prize their gems of beauty;
> Cling to gilded toys of dust;
> Boast of wealth, and fame, and pleasure;
> Only Jesus will I trust.
>
> Since mine eyes were fixed on Jesus,
> I've lost sight of all beside;
> So enchained my spirit's vision,
> Looking at the Crucified.
> —Mary D. James.

Invisible by Divine Investiture

And the loftiness of man shall be bowed down, and the haughtiness of men shall be made low: and the Lord alone shall be exalted . . . (Isa. 2:17).

A NOVICE is a person who is inclined to take credit to himself for what the Lord did through him." It is for this reason that God is hindered in His trusting us with large results. The instant we are favored with His blessing, we are like the little girl who was given a new watering can. Delighted, she ran out to the garden and began to water the flower bed. Then it began to rain. Large drops fell, but the little girl was not pleased at all and her face fell. Looking up at the raindrops for a few minutes, she exclaimed, "Mummy, doesn't God know I've got a watering can now?"

This reminds us of an evangelist who boasted that he was intending to hold services in Europe, and that he expected to beat St. Peter's record of three thousand converts. Man struts about, proud of his few drops of blessing, striving in vain to compete with God's copious showers. How much like the little girl and her watering can, when we compare man's puny efforts with a God-sent cloud-burst of revival blessing!

Torrey said: "Oh, how many a man has been full of promise and God has used him, and then that man thought that he was the whole thing and God was compelled to set him aside! I believe more promising workers have gone on the rocks through self-sufficiency and self-esteem than through any other cause.

"I can look back for forty years, or more, and think of many men who are now wrecks or derelicts who at one time the world thought were going to be something great. But they have disappeared entirely from the public view. Why? Because of over-estimation of self."

25

I knew a youth of large and lofty soul,
A soul aflame with heavenly purpose high;
Like a young eagle's, his clear, earnest eye,
Fixed on the sun, could choose no lesser goal.
For truth he lived; and love, a burning coal
From God's high altar, did the fire supply
That flushed his cheeks as morning tints the sky,
And kept him pure by its Divine control.

Lately I saw him, smooth and prosperous,
Of portly presence and distinguished air.
The cynic's smile of self-content was there,
The very air about him breathed success.
Yet by the eyes of love, too plainly seen,
Appeared the wreck of what he might have been.

— Unknown.

Alexander Maclaren has said that the reason why so few people are anointed with the Holy Ghost for service is that "so few are willing to be made invisible by the Divine investiture." It is only when we take the low place before God and are able to count ourselves as nothing, that the Holy Spirit is able to use us.

Humility is a kind of large-mindedness. The humble man grows in knowledge and power and usefulness. He takes a large and free and happy view of life. He refuses to become the victim of slights and annoyances and hostilities. He will not confine his soul to beat its wings against the cage of his self-esteem.

But the proud man is thwarted at every turn. He will not go forward that way because he has been slighted. He will not go forward another way because he must change his mind. So he stands still, and from being a man becomes a mouse.

Thus it comes to pass that "whosoever exalteth himself shall be abased; and he that humbleth himself shall be exalted." — *Treasure Chest.*

God's Exchequer to the Lowly

Blessed are the poor in spirit: for theirs is the kingdom of heaven (Matt. 5:3).

BLESSED are the poor in spirit. . . . The whole exchequer of God shall be made over by deed of gift to the soul which is humble enough to be able to receive it without growing proud because of it.

God blesses us all up to the full measure and extremity of what it is safe for Him to do. If you do not get a blessing, it is because it is not safe for you to have one. If our heavenly Father were to let your unhumbled spirit win a victory in His holy war, you would pilfer the crown for yourself, and meeting with a fresh enemy you would fall a victim, so that you are kept low for your own safety.

When a man is sincerely humble and never ventures to touch so much as a grain of praise, there is scarcely any limit to what God will do for him. Humility makes us ready to be blessed by the God of all grace, and fits us to deal efficiently with our fellow-men. — C. H. Spurgeon.

Alexander Duff, a well-known missionary and educator, remarked: "The only thing that really distresses me is that they are already publishing all manner of extravagancies about me in the newspapers. The natural tendency of all this on my spirit is to paralyze it, as the glory is too much taken from the Creator and bestowed on the creature. This is sinful, and the Holy and jealous God will not allow it, but blast the whole with the mildew of His sore displeasure. Oh for grace, grace, grace!"

Every act
Which shunned the trifling plaudits of mankind,
Shall here to wondering millions be displayed,
A monument of grace. — C. P. Layard.

"Love of glory can only create a great hero; contempt of it, a great man," said Talleyrand. And with the maxim as our rule, we might well conclude that Luther was indeed a great man however others might have judged him.

At Wittenberg, Melancthon had issued an order that all the students should rise when Luther entered to lecture. Although this was an ancient college custom, yet the humble Luther was not pleased with it, and said, "I wish Philip would give up this old fashion. These marks of honor always compel me to offer more prayers to keep me humble. If I dared I would almost retire without having read my lecture!"

When a friend proposed to him that he should dedicate one of his writings to Jerome Ebner, a Jurist-Consult of Nuremburg, who was then in great repute, "You have too high a notion of my labors," answered Luther, modestly, "but I myself have a very poor opinion of them. It was my wish, however, to comply with your desire. I looked among all my papers — which I never before thought so meanly of — I could find nothing but what seemed totally unworthy of being dedicated to so distinguished a person by so humble an individual as myself." — *Table Talk.*

"I pray," Luther said on another occasion, "you leave my name alone, and not call yourselves Lutherans, but Christians. Who is Luther? My doctrine is not mine. I have not been crucified for anyone. Paul would not that anyone should call himself of Paul or of Peter, but of Christ. How then does it befit me, a miserable bag of dust and ashes, to give my name to the children of Christ? Leave, my dear friends, these party names and distinctions. Away with them all and let us call ourselves only Christians after Him from Whom our salvation comes."

> When I survey the wondrous cross
> On which the Prince of glory died,
> My richest gain I count but loss,
> And pour contempt on all my pride.
> — Isaac Watts.

Frailty Clothes Omnipotence

He was crucified through weakness, yet he liveth by the power of God (2 Cor. 13:4).
When I am weak, then am I strong (2 Cor. 12:10).

IN nature we see that all the grandest forces are best expressed through the frailest mediums. The awful energy known as electricity works most effectually through slender wires. The mighty magnetic stream is revealed in the trembling needle. Thought is not located in an organ like a man's fist, all bone and muscle: its chosen seat is the delicate brain, and it best acts through fairy cells and attenuated films compared with which the gossamer is coarse. Life does not reside in the massive skeleton, but pulses along the silver cord of alarming delicacy.

This principle comes out supremely in Christianity — the cross is its last and highest expression. The aspect of frailty clothes omnipotence. "He was crucified through weakness, yet he liveth by the power of God." In the moment of His utmost weakness, Christ had the consciousness of measureless power and the full assurance of victory. "Thinkest thou that I cannot beseech my Father, and He shall even now send me more than twelve legions of angels?" Let us more fully understand our Master's greatness, and we shall share His confidence and peace.

The Church of God is the theater of disappointment and failure. Nothing here seems to succeed. Workers are snatched away when most wanted; expensive undertakings born in enthusiasm are buried with tears; missions starting in poetry die into prose; we are distressed on every side by delay and disaster. There is more failure with us than anywhere else. We suffer more defeats than any army. Our shipwrecks exceed those of the high seas. There would be a panic on the Stock

Exchange every day if our bankruptcies were commercial. And all this implies our glory.

The sense of failure is acutest where the aim is highest, and the catalog of defeats suggests the grandeur of the enterprise. Think of the enemies we challenge: our vast ambition, our immense field of action, the difficult elements in which we work, and no wonder that we know most of the sense of failure, and feel failure most keenly.

But our failures are infinite successes, our defeats — victories, our martyrs — conquerors; we faint only to prevail, we die to live in resurrection power and beauty. . . . He Who is the same yesterday, today, and forever, knows all this. It is His own program, and He is not disheartened. — W. L. Watkinson.

> By failure and defeat made wise,
>   We come to know, at length,
> What strength within our weakness lies,
>   What weakness in our strength.
>
> What inward peace is born of strife;
>   What power of being spent;
> What wings unto our upward life
>   Is noble discontent.
>
> O Lord, we need Thy shaming look
>   That burns all low desire;
> The discipline of Thy rebuke
>   Shall be refining fire!
>   — Frederic Lucian Hosner.

Our Lord died an apparent failure, discredited by the leaders of established religion, rejected by society, and forsaken by His friends. The man who ordered Him to the cross was the successful statesman whose hand the ambitious hack politician kissed. It took the Resurrection to demonstrate how gloriously Christ had triumphed and how tragically the governor had failed. — A. W. Tozer.

Reigning by Serving

He that loveth his life shall lose it; and he that hateth his life in this world shall keep it unto life eternal (John 12:25).

A PARADOX has been defined thus: "A tenet or proposition contrary to received opinion and seemingly absurd, but true in fact."

The Gospel of Christ is full of paradoxes, for God's thoughts and ways are on a higher plane than human thoughts and ways, and therefore appear impossible and even absurd from the merely human standpoint, just as the statements and actions of an astronomer searching the heavens with a telescope would appear absurd to the wild savages in the heart of Africa. We give a few of these paradoxes:

We see unseen things (2 Cor. 4:18).
We conquer by yielding (Matt. 5:5), (Rom. 12:20,21).
We rest under a yoke (Matt. 11:28-30).
We reign by serving (Mark 10:42,44).
We become great by becoming little (Matt 18:4).
We are exalted by being humbled (Matt. 23:12).
We become wise by becoming foolish (1 Cor. 1:20,21).
We become free by becoming slaves (Rom. 6:17-22), (Rom. 8:2).
We possess all things by having nothing (2 Cor. 6:10).
All things are ours because we are not our own (1 Cor. 3:21), (1 Cor. 6:19).
When we are weak then we are strong (2 Cor. 12:10).
We triumph by defeat (2 Cor. 12:7-9).
Our honor is in our shame (Phil. 2:5-11), (Luke 6:26).
We glory in our infirmities (2 Cor. 12:5).
We live by dying (John 12:24,25), (2 Cor. 4:10,11).
— *Bright Words, 1902-1907.*

"You will shine the brighter," said Shelhamer, a minister and author, "by giving up your own brilliancy; go the faster by walking softly with your God; grow eternally tall by sitting on a low bench; reign over others by letting them reign over you; yea, save your life by losing it."

Make me a captive, Lord,
    And then I shall be free;
Force me to render up my sword,
    And I shall conqu'ror be.
I sink in life's alarms
    When by myself I stand;
Imprison me within Thine arms,
    And strong shall be my hand.

My heart is weak and poor
    Until it master find;
It has no spring of action sure—
    It varies with the wind.
It cannot freely move,
    Till Thou hast wrought its chain;
Enslave it with Thy matchless love,
    And deathless it shall reign.

My will is not my own
    Till Thou hast made it Thine;
If it would reach a monarch's throne
    It must its crown resign;
It only stands unbent
    Amid the crashing strife,
When on Thy bosom it has leant
    And found in Thee its life.
                    —George Matheson.

Water Seeks the Lowest Level

But where shall wisdom be found? and where is the place of understanding? When he made a decree for the rain, and a way for the lightning of the thunder (Job 28:12,26).

LILIAS Trotter, an English woman of promising artistic talent, gave up all worldly prospects and went out to North Africa as a missionary with two other companions. All were in ill health; they knew no one on the field; none of them were acquainted with the language. They had a God too big to fail them.

Lilias Trotter was a great student of nature, and learning the laws that govern that realm, she applied these same laws to the spiritual realm. She received great comforting from God's word to Job and comments thus on the above verses:

"...God finds the way for the wind and the waters and the lightning. It came with a blessed power what those ways are:

"The way for the wind is in the region of the greatest emptiness.

"The way for the water is to the place of the greatest depth.

"The way for the lightning is along the line of the greatest weakness. 'If any man lack.' There is God's condition for His inflow of the spiritual understanding. . . .

"In our northern lands a watercourse shows out as the richest green of the meadow land, broken by a ripple and a glimmer and a glitter through reeds and ferns and moss. Not such are the African watercourses, and not such are God's counterparts in the spiritual kingdom.

"Out here you can detect the channel by the clue that it will be the barest of the bare places — sun-bleached, rounded stones, stretching across a plain or a deep cut gulley winding among the tablelands that bind the Sahara to the North.

"But summer and winter you will see in those barren waterways a supply going down to the oasis that cluster among the cliffs and bastions where the plateau breaks down to the desert. Trace the gulley upwards till it is but a trench, and you will probably find that it starts with a scooped-out hollow in the gravel no more than a couple of feet across, holding a pool that shows a bubble now and then. In that pool lies the source of life for the oasis down below.

"The water begins by grooving that trench at the lowest level it can find, and it seeks all the time to make that level lower still, carving for itself at last a veritable ravine till it has reached the mission that was the meaning of the lonely path, of the stripping bare of the ever-deepening emptiness. For the last sweep of its ravine has sent it forth into the glory of its mission. Away beyond stretched thousands upon thousands of palm trees, waiting for the treasure that the water course has brought down. The power of the water and the laying low of the channel — between them they have opened this great gateway. 'Thou didst cleave the earth with Thy rivers.'

"So with ourselves, instead of a life of conscious power, ours will probably, if He is going to do any deep work in us, be a path of humiliation, of stripping, of emptiness, where no flesh may glory in His presence.

"The way goes downward and downward into the valley of humiliation as the self-life stands gradually revealed by God's presence! On and on, instead of the sense of power, there comes only more and more the overwhelming sense of insufficiency — for in the spiritual, as in the natural world, if you want to seek water, look in the very lowest place that you can find. Whatever the ministry may be, it is the same story, the stream-bed going lower and lower, with nothing to glory in but the wonderful glory of bearing the life-giving water. 'Death worketh in us, but life in you,' the water courses say.

"Yes, the way 'goes downward and downward,' while natural man's whole tendency is to raise himself in arrogant pride."

Hollow out your heart by self-distrust, and God will fill it with the flashing waters of His strength bestowed. — Unknown.

Lowliness the Goal

I was brought low, and he helped me (Psa. 116:6).

MALCOLM Muggeridge was a searcher after truth for many years. In the course of this search, he traveled to Russia in order to explore the possibilities of Communism, only to be bitterly disappointed and disillusioned. Finally, he found in Christ the End of his search and exhorts us thus:

"Let us as Christians rejoice that we see around us on every hand the decay of the institutions and instruments of power; intimations of empires falling to pieces, money in total disarray, dictators and parliamentarians alike nonplussed by the confusion and conflicts which encompass them.

"For it is precisely when every earthly hope has been explored and found wanting, when every possibility of help from earthly sources has been sought and is not forthcoming, when every recourse this world offers, moral as well as material, has been explored to no effect, when in the shivering cold the last faggot has been thrown on the fire and in the gathering darkness every glimmer of light has finally flickered out – it is then that Christ's hand reaches out, sure and firm, that Christ's words bring their inexpressible comfort, that His light shines brightest, abolishing the darkness forever. So, finding in everything only deception and nothingness, the soul is constrained to have recourse to God Himself and to rest content with Him."

George Fox, the founder of the Quaker movement, was brought to see this amazing truth: "When all my hopes in all men were gone, so that I had nothing outwardly to help me, then, oh, then, I heard a voice which said, 'There is One, even Christ Jesus, that can speak to thy condition,' and, when I heard it, my heart did leap for joy."

C. A. Fox, yet another Englishman and one of the first speakers at the Keswick Convention, reiterates the Scriptural truth that when we are brought low we find help: "We learn who it is whom the Lord helps: 'It is those who are brought low.' We thought it was when we were getting on, showing pluck, keeping up to a good place, that the Lord helped. But now we know something deeper, that those who are saved are the sinful ones: that it is not those who are wise, and not many who are noble, but the fools and the despised whom God hath chosen. 'Father, I thank Thee, that Thou hast hid these things from the wise and prudent, and hast revealed them unto babes!'

"You little thought that was the way to Heaven! You thought it was through shining lights, the avenues of angels, but He has shown you now that it is by the dark stair of sorrow that He helped you when brought very low. Oh, blessed be God for the dark stair which leads us down to His Heaven!"

Thy home is with the humble, Lord!
The simplest are the best;
Thy lodging is in childlike hearts;
Thou makest there Thy rest.

Dear Comforter! Eternal Love!
If Thou wilt stay with me,
Of lowly thoughts, and simple ways
I'll build a house for Thee.

Who made this beating heart of mine
But Thou, my heavenly Guest?
Let no one have it, then, but Thee,
And let it be Thy rest.
— *Lyra Catholica.*

God has two thrones — the one in the highest heavens, the other in the lowliest hearts. — Unknown.

The Tragedy of the Self-Sufficient

Not that we are sufficient of ourselves to think any thing as of ourselves; but our sufficiency is of God (2 Cor. 3:5).

I HAPPENED to pick up a copy of a magazine a while ago, and I noticed an article which was called "Ten Ways To Get Rid of Fear." What a title! So I started reading. I guessed pretty well what the man would have to say, but I thought I would have a look. It was the usual stuff written by a psychiatrist.

In the last of the ten points, he said, "Have faith." And I pricked up my mental ears for a moment, and then turned over the page. It continued, "Have faith in yourself. You've gone through before, you've struggled through in the past, you'll get through again." You may smile . . . but there's an ache in my heart, and that is no exaggeration. That is the tragedy of modern philosophy — self-sufficiency.

The fact is that I am poor and desperately needy. There is a sense in which I want the Lord never to take me off my knees, for it is when I am there, that I am in the place of miracles. I am destitute. This was David's conviction about himself. He said, "I am poor and needy." . . .

You should have seen some of the brilliant ideas I had in order to try to reach men for Christ. They were terrific, smashing, legion. But — one by one, gadgets, gimmicks, and all — they fell apart. They were useless, hopeless, and I found there was only one way. I am so ashamed that the eventide of my life has come and I have used it so seldom. And that way is when I am flat on my face before the Lord and say, "Lord, it is up to You. I am helpless and destitute."

Destitute! Destitute! Destitute! That is where I have to get in my life and program and service. After I had been in Chicago for five years, a man rang me up from a church board in New Jersey and said, "Pastor Redpath, our church is without a pastor. Do you know anybody who would fill the pulpit?" I mentioned three or four men whom I knew.

He asked me everything under the sun about their education—what university did they attend, what degrees did they have? What about their families? When he ceased the long conversation of about fifty minutes, he said, "Thank you so much for telling me about these men. It is very good of you, but you know, none of them are big enough for our pulpit." I hope he didn't think I was rude, but I could not let him go without saying, "Sir, are you sure you do not mean they are not small enough?"

I tell you, my friend, if you are a Christian leader, or in the pulpit, or singing, or teaching a Sunday School class, or if you are doing anything for the Lord—it isn't the big shot, the big man that God wants—it's the broken man. God uses the man whom He has crushed until he is nothing but a door mat for people to walk on in order that they might come to Jesus. . . .

I honestly believe that one of the curses of twentieth century evangelical Christianity is that we are not destitute. We've become desperately self-sufficient. Indeed, so great is the craze for higher education that we train young people today to be self-sufficient, to major in the things in which they will succeed—to be a big shot.

I'm not saying anything about education. Get the very best you can, but I want to remind you of what Paul said about self-sufficiency. Paul was a man of outstanding education, the brilliant theologian of his day, and he said, "Our sufficiency is of God." Two thousand years have gone by and the situation is no different. Our sufficiency, our help, our hope is not in programs, not in a theological degree—not in anything but the Lord! —Alan Redpath.

Faith is dependence upon God. And this God-dependence only begins when self-dependence ends. And self-dependence only comes to its end, with some of us, when sorrow, suffering, affliction, broken plans and hopes bring us to that place of self-helplessness and defeat.

—James H. McConkey.

38

Need Determines Supply

*Joy shall be in heaven over one sinner that repenteth, more than over ninety-and-nine just persons, which **need no repentance** (Luke 15:7).*

A MAN'S own need is the measure of his greatness.
— Pascal.

"No need?" How tragic! The Psalmist again and again speaks of himself as being "poor and needy." That is why God speaks of David as a man after His own heart. The full Christ sends empty away, but the hungry are satisfied, and the thirsty are refreshed, and the needy take of His fullness.

Jesus had been criticized by the Pharisees for eating with publicans and sinners, and the entire fifteenth chapter of Luke is Christ's answer to that criticism. The sheep that was lost demanded the Shepherd's care so that He left the ninety-nine who needed nothing. The woman who had lost her coin rejoiced when she found it. The prodigal is but the story of every soul who in fullness goes into a far country. It is always a far country when we leave the Father and venture on our own. It is always riotous living when we walk after the flesh, living only for that which is passing and thus missing that which is eternal and enduring.

Like the prodigal, our true success story begins when we first feel the pinch and "begin to be in want" when "no man gives unto us." It is only then we come to ourselves and realize that in the Father's house is bread enough and to spare while we perish with hunger amidst the world's seeming fullness. The elder brother had no need. He lived in the midst of His Father's plenty, and all that the Father had was his as well, but his self-sufficiency and self-righteousness blocked the inflow of love to his flinty heart.

Blessed day, when those things in which we trusted are snatched from us. We call it tragedy. God calls it blessedness.

He makes His promises to needy people — those who hunger and thirst for righteousness are filled. Christ uses the picture of hunger and thirst for they are universal, ever-recurring needs. No wonder He could say they were blessed, for they more often partook of the Living Christ Who was the Bread of Life. Eating His flesh and drinking His blood were the only means of LIFE. "He that cometh to me shall never hunger, and he that believeth on me shall never thirst."

Christ used the picture of the Vine to illustrate to us the importance of need. What is it that causes the branch to receive sap from the parent stem? Osmosis — need! The branch's need calls on the vine for a supply of sap, and lo, it is supplied. More need! More supply!

Blessed bereavement which casts me for companionship upon Jesus. Blessed bankruptcy which causes me to rest on Eternal Resources instead of the riches that have wings and fly away. Blessed ill health that flings me upon the mighty virtue and healing that comes from Jesus, the Great Physician. Blessed failure in my ministry which at last reveals to me that my own efforts are unavailing and my best works ephemeral. Blessed collapse of all self-confidence, for I now have the all-sufficient One, Who came to be my life, my wisdom, my sanctification, my redemption, and most of all, my righteousness. — J. R. Miller.

> God lets us go our way alone,
>   Till we are homesick and distressed,
> And humbly then come back to own
>   His way is best.
>
> He lets us thirst by Horeb's rock,
>   And hunger in the wilderness;
> Yet, at our feeblest, faintest knock,
>   He waits to bless.
>
> He lets us faint in far-off lands,
>   And feed on husks and feel the smart,
> Till we come home with empty hands,
>   And swelling heart.
>   — J. R. Miller.

Divine Diminishing

And the Lord said unto Gideon, The people that are with thee are too many for me to give the Midianites into their hands, lest Israel vaunt themselves against me, saying, Mine own hand hath saved me (Judges 7:2).

SOMEONE has declared, "A man may be too big for God to use but he cannot be too little." This comes as a shock in an age of extreme bigness. Everything is bigger and more ambitious than ever before. Advocated on all fronts are mergers and artificial swelling processes to give weight and power, or at least an appearance of them.

God's good old Bible shows a principle of divine success that is the exact antithesis of all this. God must, in His servants, find smallness, nothingness, humility, and dependence. Where He does not detect these, He may have to reject the applicant altogether. If, however, He sees even the slightest flickering desire to be humbly used of God, the Divine Master-maker will put the candidate through a whittling process that he will never in the hour of victory say those chest-expanding, but God-dishonoring words, "I did it." More important is the provision through the Cross whereby the old Adam can be crucified with Christ so that it is not "I" but Christ Who lives and labors from that hour.

The reading of the Old Testament is fascinating because of the Divine Diminishing. Much of its charm is the relation of tremendous accomplishments with very small instruments. A word, a rod, a lamp and pitcher, a sling and five stones, and lo, marvelous feats, out of all proportion to the size of the visible instrument, are forthcoming. And so as all human instruments are the largest available, there must be a drastic reduction before God can employ them.

David had simple faith in God but no doubt there was a danger of too much success and popularity going to his head. Saul offered him his own armor with which to combat the giant but God gave him such a feeling of insecurity with all that big armory that he reduced himself to his sling and five smooth stones, plus his faith in God. Then, to the accompanying tune of the most sarcastic and taunting slurs concerning his youth and his littleness and his "light artillery," a platform was furnished from which God could get all the glory for the victory.

And Gideon had his army numbered at forty-two thousand men. But what were they against the Midianites who covered the land with their multitude! It took plenty of faith, one would say, for Gideon's army to think of defeating the enemy with a so much larger army. But God was taking no chances with the natural pride of man, so He reduced it first to ten thousand and then to a laughable little party of three hundred, plus lamps and pitchers and a God-taught, God-honoring slogan. And the victory came!

Often we hear at the end of a prayer petition, those good words, "And we shall be careful to give God the glory." But we can never do this without God's diminishing process. That process is co-crucifixion by faith with Jesus on the Cross. The old Adam is always big and aspiring to be bigger. When Jesus died, rose again, and ascended into glory He left a pathetic little pack of failures—mainly humble fishermen, who had aspired to be "the greatest in the Kingdom." They had coveted the places of honor on the right and left of the Master when He would come into His kingdom. The future of Christianity appeared hopeless in their hands, but after Pentecost they were so small that one fails to see them as the actors at all— they were little men with a great God. And their tools were as insignificant as their stature in the sight of the world.

Since Pentecost, God's instruments have become nothing through Calvary. They have learned that willpower or any other human force can never make a man small enough to be able at all times to let God have all the glory. It is a precious moment when a weary soul asks earnestly and in faith, "Lord, let me be nothing; let me die with Thee." —E. F. Harvey.

God's Mighty Minority

The flight shall perish from the swift, and the strong shall not strengthen his force, neither shall the mighty deliver himself (Amos 2:14).

GOD has always blessed quality rather than quantity in the promotion of His cause. He seeks not men but a man. Never has He been impressed or depressed by numbers, equipment, and ability. Never has He been impressed or depressed by personality, prestige, or popularity. Much of what we call wisdom is sheer foolishness with God. Some jobs may depend on what you know, but the work of God depends upon Whom you know. You must know God.

As far as God is concerned there are no "big men" in His work, for He putteth down one and setteth up another. He inspects rather than respects our person. Fact is — humanity must be reduced to practically nothing before it can be induced to do much of anything for Heaven. When a person feels he has nothing, is worth nothing, and can do nothing, aside from Divine assistance, he is eligible for membership in the ranks of God's "mighty minority."

It matters little what you have so long as you have God; it matters little where you have been so long as you have been to Calvary; it matters little whom you know as long as you know God; it matters little what you possess as long as you are possessed of the Holy Ghost.

God has been known to use a stick in the hand of Moses, a stone in the sling of David, and a staff in the hand of Benaiah. He used vermin to move Pharaoh, as ass to move Baalam, and a fish to move Jonah. His equipment is inexhaustible, and His methods of labor innumerable. All He needs is a yielded instrument.

History usually marks the man who has made a mark for God. Those who have succeeded in surrendering to God the whole man have been known throughout the whole world.

Too many are waiting for God to move upon them, when they ought to be prevailing upon Him. We may all sing, "God is still on the Throne," but I wonder who is sitting upon yours? He stood in honor of His faithful martyr, Stephen, and, no doubt, would stand more often if we gave Him occasion to do so.

It is not a matter of whether or not we have numbers — but do we have God? Someone has said, "If God be for us, what difference does it make who is against us?" Anyone plus God is a sufficiency. Some of history's greatest conflicts have been decided by a minority of men in the hands of Divinity. — George Bowen.

As for me my bed is made: I am against bigness and greatness in all their forms, and (am) with the invisible, molecular, moral forces that work from individual to individual, stealing in through the crannies of the world, like so many soft rootlets, or like the capillary oozing of water, and yet rending the hardest monuments of man's pride, if you give them time.

I am against all big organizations as such, national ones first and foremost; against all big successes and big results, and in favor of the eternal forces of truth which always work in the individual... underdogs always, till history comes, after they are long dead, and puts them on top. — From *The Letters of William James.*

F. A. Schaeffer years later reiterates the truth of William James and George Bowen: "Nowhere more than in America are Christians caught in the twentieth-century syndrome of size. Size will show success. If I am consecrated there will necessarily be large quantities of people, dollars, etc. This is not so. Not only does God not say that size and spiritual power go together, but He even reverses this and tells us to be deliberately careful not to choose a place too big for us. We all tend to emphasize big words and important places, but all such emphasis is of the flesh. To think in such terms is simply to hearken back to the old, unconverted, egoistic, self-centered me."

When Weakness Is Dynamite

Out of weakness were made strong (Heb. 11:34).

W. B. Godbey, an old-time revivalist and an excellent Greek scholar, was much used of God in his travels, and his constant petition to Conference was that he would be sent to the hardest and most difficult field of labor. He shares with us a secret he had learned from communion with the Almighty:

"I am an old revivalist. We always had to have a repetition of Gethsemane and Calvary before we could reach the triumphant resurrection and the glorious ascension. On arrival, finding all elated over the new evangelist and shouting over the revival in sight, I knew that we had to get rid of great carloads of human lumber and trash before we could see the glory of God. Soon my plain, hard, rough preaching and earnest crying to God would disgust them, so all their hopes would evanesce, and giving up all expectation of a revival, they would be very sorry they had called me, feeling it was the mistake of their lives.

"Then came the salient point of the campaign. Frequently at that epoch they would run me off, of course defeating the enterprise outright. When they bore with me in utter desperation, all blue as indigo, feeling that it was infinitely worse than a failure, they all got out of the way and I was out of the way, because they were all disgusted with me. When we reached that significant crisis, a shout always began in the deep interior of my heart, because I knew victory was at hand.

"I never knew a failure when all human resources and hopes evanesced away. When we reached the place of nothing but insults, destitutions, weakness, persecutions, and tight places for Christ's sake, then the dynamite came and blew down the walls of Jericho, burst the devil's kingdom, revealed the glory of God and the victories of Christ on all sides to the unutterable surprise of everybody.

"In many cases when they all so fell out with me that I had no home, but stood for days and weeks alone with Jesus, preaching the truth fearless of men and devils, unearthing all the hidden things of darkness, exposing all Satan's refuges of lies, cutting every cable with the sword of the Spirit, after the power came and the tide swept over everything, they almost pulled me to pieces to take me to their home.

"Depend upon it as a maxim, never letting it slip: 'When I am without strength then am I dynamite.' Our resources, power, and hope must evacuate the field before omnipotent grace can glorify God. Poor humanity must get out of the way before the power and glory of God can be revealed. The reason why we don't have revivals everywhere after the Pentecostal style is because we have too much power, too many resources, and too much encouragement. You will never see the glory of God till all this gets out of the way.

"'But we have this treasure in earthen vessels, in order that the excellency of the power may be of God, and not of us' (2 Cor. 4:7). All the splendor, pomp, pageantry, gold, silver, and adornment appertaining to the priesthood, tabernacle, and temple of the former dispensation had been entirely eliminated, not a vestige surviving. Hence the folly and impertinency of filling the world with it during the Gospel ages. It was all symbolic in its day and passed away with all the types and shadows superseded by the glorious Antitype. Hence the Gospel ministry is all in the valley of humiliation. . . . Whenever we bring in human power, learning, wealth, and influence, we thereby put a veil over the popular mind, disqualifying them to see the Invisible One. . . .

"In every subsequent age, when human power, wealth, and culture come to the front, we see the Holy Spirit retreat away, leaving them to run their own machinery, and, pursuant to first principles, picking up others — poor, weak, and uninfluential — from the low places of the earth, and sending them out, the custodians of this invaluable Heavenly treasure. God is not going to change His Gospel economy to suit any of us, giving His glory to another. The humiliation of the Gospel is here exemplified by the Apostles themselves, down at the very bottom of society, the contempt of the world's elite."

The Kingdom of the Lowly

My kingdom is not of this world: if my kingdom were of this world then would my servants fight . . . but now is my kingdom not from hence (John 18:36).

HOW hard does each one of us find it to learn that fundamental law of the kingdom of God, that it is only he that humbleth himself that shall be exalted. 'For the meek shall inherit the earth.'

"How then, I ask again, has Christ attained to His sovereignty, seeing that He has gained it neither by inheritance nor by conquest? Oh, it was in a way the most unlike what worldly men would dream of, a way which no man can understand, excepting him to whom it has been taught by the Spirit of God! 'Whosoever will be great among you, let him be your minister. And whosoever will be chief among you, let him be your servant. Even as the Son of man came not to be ministered unto, but to minister, and to give his life a ransom for many.' What a strange, unheard-of way is this to a throne and a crown! Other men who would hold a scepter would come in power; He came in weakness; others would substantiate their claim to authority; He laid His aside. . . .

"Then again, no man can with carnal weapons conquer for himself the kingdom of God. It is true, in all other things, that in proportion as a man has wealth and power, strength of body, and force of character, does the world and all it contains lie at his feet. Everything is in his power; everything may become his, saving one, and that is the kingdom of God. In that kingdom, very different laws come into operation. The poor have the Gospel preached to them that they may be satisfied, while the rich must suffer want. He putteth down the mighty from their seats and exalteth them of low degree. Men are overthrown, and little children receive the kingdom. How many of the first shall be last, and of the last, first! And will Christ administer His government in the time to come in another way, according to other laws, than He does now?

47

Here He was not surrounded by the powerful and the wise, according to the flesh, but by what men would call the foolish and weak of the world. He will keep the word which He hath spoken. He will confess none before His heavenly Father but those who have confessed Him, with word and heart, before men.

"Here we may even go further. So far from its being the case that reputation and riches, beauty and talents, by which everything else may be acquired, make the entrance to the kingdom more easy; these things rather make it more difficult. 'How hardly shall they that have riches.'. . . For the richer a man is, the more is he disposed to be self-satisfied, and the more difficult is it for him to practice self-denial. 'Strait is the gate, and narrow is the way, that leadeth into life,' says our Lord. And it is just because the gate is so strait and the way so narrow that all the riches a man brings with him must be left outside. . . .

"And thus times may come in which the kingdom of God . . . even throughout the universal Church, is a kingdom invisible in the eyes of men; but all the more in such times will the members there which still live manifest the life they have, should their only symptom of vitality be their antagonism against those members which are dead. . . . The kingdom of God is no mere idea of man, but an eternal thought of God."

The above has been translated from a sermon by Frederick A. Tholuck given at the University of Halle. This hall of learning had drifted far from that spiritual life which it had enjoyed under Spener, Franke, etc. Tholuck born in 1799 had seemed to come to the kingdom for such a time as this, and filled the chair of Theology for fifty-one years. His biographer says, "It was no easy place into which Tholuck entered when he accepted the call. He found Halle a hotbed of rationalism, and was strongly opposed by his colleagues, including the great Hebrew scholar, Gesenius. . . . Out of a student body of nine hundred, only five could be found who believed in the deity of Christ! Yet such was the influence of this man of God that the complexion of Halle was completely changed, and the university became a noted center of Evangelicalism."

—From *Light From the Cross*.

No Righteousness of Our Own

And be found in him, not having mine own righteousness, which is of the law, but that which is through the faith of Christ, the righteousness which is of God by faith (Phil. 3:9).

IF our hands that should grasp the heavenly treasures are kept closed with earthly things, deal with us, Lord, until we stretch out empty hands, suppliants for Thy blessings.
— Andrew Bonar.

During our ministry, we have found it difficult to dislodge people from a position of resting satisfied because of some wonderful experience they have had in the past. Perhaps it was a born-again experience; perhaps it was sanctification; perhaps it was some wonderful gift they received from God. These all were necessary at one time in their lives, but they had stopped in their journey. They felt that they had arrived. They looked backwards to some blessing, rather than forward to all Christ had for them. They were dwelling on the past rather than enjoying a present touch from God.

Oswald Chambers in *Bringing Sons unto Glory,* says: "May God save us from the selfish meanness of a sanctified life which says, 'I am saved and sanctified; look what a wonderful specimen I am.' If we are saved and sanctified we have lost sight of ourselves absolutely. Self is effaced; it is not there. The sacrifice of the sanctified self is the lesson to be learned. We are saved and sanctified for God, not to be specimens for His showroom, but for God to do with us as He did with Jesus, make us broken bread and poured out wine as He chooses. That is the test—not spiritual fireworks, or hysterics, not fanaticism, but a blazingly holy life that 'confronts the horror of the world with a fierce purity,' chaste physically, morally, and spiritually, and this only comes about in the way it came about in the life of our Lord."

A. B. Simpson had some wonderful experiences with Christ, but he came to the place where his hands were so full of this past spiritual history that he could not receive present, moment-by-moment blessings: "I went to meetings and heard people speak of joy. I even thought I had the joy, but I did not keep it because I had not Himself as my joy. At last He said to me—Oh, so tenderly—'My child, just take Me and let Me be in you the constant supply of all this, Myself.' And when at last I got my eyes off my sanctification, and my experience of it, and placed them on the Christ in me, I found, instead of an experience, I had a Christ larger than the moment's need, the Christ that had all that I should ever need, Who was given to me at once and forever!

"And when I thus saw Him, it was such rest: it was all right, and right for ever. For I had not only what I could hold that little hour, but all that I should need the next and the next and so on. . . ."

John Wesley, whom many have misunderstood in his teaching of Christian Perfection, saw the dangers which arose from Christians resting on the experience as an "it" rather than on Christ. He said: "That moment I cease to look to Christ I am all unholiness." The devil is always attempting to stifle the Christ-life within, and he often does this by taking every emotional feeling, every experience, every gift of God, and perverting them. He knows only too well that a Christian will inevitably stalemate if he rests upon a past experience rather than on a moment-by-moment faith in Christ.

My goal is God Himself, not joy, nor peace,
  Nor even blessing, but Himself, my God:
'Tis His to lead me there, not mine, but His—
  "At any cost, dear Lord, by any road!"
— F. Brook.

The Opiate of Self-Satisfaction

Not as though I had already attained, either were already perfect: but I follow after, if that I may apprehend that for which also I am apprehended of Christ Jesus. Brethren, I count not myself to have apprehended: but this one thing I do, forgetting those things which are behind, and reaching forth unto those things which are before, I press toward the mark for the prize of the high-calling of God in Christ Jesus (Phil. 3:12-14).

THE tragedy of the Pharisee was this—he had finally attained; all his riches were in possession: he had arrived. Pharisaism had a jeweler's window; it had no mines. It spent its time in window-dressing; it never set out on wondering explorations. But the Lord Jesus has created an ideal of character, and has opened out dim and enticing vistas of possibility which leave us, after every conquest, with new dominions yet to be won. Every summit brings a new revelation, the reward of every attainment is a vision of further glory. And so it happens that, altogether unlike Pharisaism, in the ranks of the Lord's disciples the best are the lowliest; those who are furthest up the slopes are the least conscious of their attainments, for they contemplate, with breathless reverence, the far-spreading glories of their "unsearchable riches" in Christ. —J. H. Jowett in *The Silver Lining*.

> Hints haunt me ever of a More beyond;
> I am rebuked by a sense of the incomplete,
> Of a completion oversoon assumed—
> Of adding up too soon.
>   —Unknown.

One of the fundamental shortcomings of the evangelicals is the general spiritual attitude: "I have obtained." Such an attitude stifles spiritual ambition for higher things and greater perfection. A child must grow and grow until he reaches maturity, but having reached maturity, the child, now a man or woman, must continue to grow in mental, moral, and spiritual status. If a child at the age of twelve or fourteen should say, "I have attained, I have come as far as I want to come," and somehow by wishful thinking could stop his growth, what a dwarfed product the child would be!

Now, this is exactly true about most Christians today; they have reached a certain state — have had one or two Christian experiences, and then they have become smug and complacent. They have now stopped growing, and thus the churches are full of dwarfed Christians who have stopped in their spiritual progress. They believe that they have reached the final goal of Christian perfection. They may vehemently deny this attitude in words, but their whole life and attitude eloquently reveal this. There is no stretching out for higher ground — no striving for greater achievements. Because of this mental level of the Church, nothing extraordinary happens.

The feeling that one has attained is the feeling of the graveyard. Those who have been buried there indeed have attained — to corruption and death. For when movement and progress ends, death and corruption begins. All great evangelical awakenings in their origin have been MOVEMENTS. And while these spiritual awakenings were "Movements," they were full of holy ambition and life-producing aspirations. They laughed at the very gates of hell, for the very gates of hell could not prevail against them! It was when these movements began to stabilize and solidify, they gradually began to fossilize and finally to petrify. The old forms have remained, but LIFE has gone out of the forms. As a rule, the "Movement" settles down to a "Church." The organism becomes an organization and the liberty of the Spirit is supplemented by the slavery of ecclesiasticism. — Basil A. Malof in *A Man in a Hurry* by James Alexander Stewart. Used by permission.

Be always displeased at what thou art, if thou desirest to attain to what thou art not, for when thou hast pleased thyself, there thou abidest. — St. Augustine.

Blessed Hay

He raiseth up the poor out of the dust, and lifteth up the beggar from the dunghill, to set them among princes, and to make them inherit the throne of glory. . . (1 Sam. 2:8).

JOHN Wright Follette has blessed many by his pungent messages and beautiful poetry. He received his inspiration for this poem, "Blessed Hay," in a camp-meeting tabernacle when the hay on the floor spoke a message to his heart. His own words best convey that inspiration:

"Do you remember the evening I took up a handful of hay as an illustration? Well, I saw not only the hay but also an object lesson of deep humility and brokenness. . . . Here it was to become the floor covering for a tabernacle. People were to tread upon it, kick it about under careless, ruthless feet, push it under their benches, kneel upon it and break it up in general. . . .

"I am telling you a little (not very much) of what I saw when I looked at the hay upon the ground. The day after the meetings closed when nearly all the people had left the grounds, I went over alone to the tabernacle and knelt down in the hay to thank God for His sweet presence during the time we fellowshiped together. He met me too, during those days and blessed me and refreshed my tired heart. Then I took up a handful of the hay and slipped it into an envelope and here it is on my desk before me—a gentle and lowly minstrel. This poem is what I hear singing in my heart:

"'O blessed hay, all broken, marred and crushed,
What happy memories must haunt thee now!
Do humming bees still move in eager quest
For sweetness hidden in thy clover heart?
Do happy birds still swing in lowly sweep
Close to thy breast upturning to the sun?

53

And do the fleeting clouds still bless with rain
Thy thirsty form stretched naked 'neath the sky?
At eventide when twilight spins her veil
Of loveliness, do gentle dews distil?
O blessed hay, what memories are thine!
Today I see thee stretched upon the ground
All dry and broken 'neath the seekers' feet,
The hungry hearts kneel upon thee now.
It is not thee they seek — not thee, not thee.
How sweet thy willingness to have it so!
It is not theirs to know thy life or heart;
What care have they for what thou might have been,
Or what thy heart may hold for days to come?
They only seek a place to rest their knees —
The cruel earth is harsh to seeking hearts.
Then, let them kneel or rest their weary forms
Upon thy broken beauty, once so dear.
Sweet waving grass in summer, sun-kissed field,
Though blest with all that nature may provide,
Is never hay till *cut* and wholly *dried*.
O blessed hay, how sacred is thy lot!
The hungry soul may kneel upon thee hard,
May mar thy form and press thee to the dust,
But you are helping them to God just now.
It matters not what form our service takes —
Just *be* the thing the Master may desire —
Yes, hay upon the tabernacle floor.'"

— Used by permission.

God is looking for broken men, for men who have judged themselves in the light of the Cross of Christ. When He wants anything done, He takes up men who have come to an end of themselves and whose trust and confidence is not in themselves but in God. — *Message from God.*

Speaking Only of Him

He that speaketh of himself seeketh his own glory: but he that seeketh his glory that sent him, the same is true, and no unrighteousness is in him (John 7:18).

MOST of us often receive brochures in the mail appealing for our prayers and financial assistance. How can we know what is genuine? The Bible is very practical in its outworkings, and a study of Scripture will give wisdom on this line. "If any man will do his will, he shall know of the doctrine, whether it be of God, or whether I speak of myself. He that speaketh of himself seeketh his own glory."

The test, then, is simple. When you listen to a preacher or open a brochure, of whom does the preacher or writer speak? Do pictures of the writer or healer adorn more than one page of the glossy magazine? Here is an opportunity of shining before the public in some new endeavor to spread the Gospel. Often the evangelist unwittingly makes merchandise of souls, using them as bait to catch the dollars that lie hidden in vaults, bonds, or bedroom. But he that advertiseth himself seeketh his own glory or the glory of his work, and this may be done even in the Christian realm. Is this work then worthy of my support? The test is easy. Of whom does the bulletin speak?

Let us notice in the Scripture God's discipline of a man who spake of himself. Job was upright and perfect in God's sight, for the book of Job says so. Yet Satan was allowed to put his slimy hands upon the fortunes of this upright man in order to test his motives. Failing in that endeavor, the devil was allowed to touch Job's body after having bereaved him of family, wealth, and honor. His three comforters interpret his impoverishment as a punishment for sin.

But although God has permitted the devilish devices of the Evil One, He uses these very circumstances to make of the upright man, a holy one. Job has been frugal, industrious, persevering, and philanthropic and therefore he justifies himself. Which of us have not been guilty of this? In chapters twenty-nine through thirty-one Job speaks of himself, using "I," "me," "mine" about 80 times. There is something which does not quite ring true in the words of this wonderful man who is being so tested. But he is to come out of his testing with a loathing for himself and a deeper devotion to the Father in Heaven.

Yes, Job had heard of Him and spoken well of Him, but it was a mixture. Until there has been a personal revelation of the holiness of God, we cannot but speak of ourselves. We may have been born again and long to reveal Christ, but self intrudes. Who is the prominent figure in the bulletin, the brochure, the magazine, the book, the sermon? The test is simple: "He that speaketh of himself seeketh his own glory."

There is a vast difference between an upright man and a holy man. One is circumspect in his outward acts of life. We call him righteous. But the holy man has by revelation seen the inward motivations of his heart. He has seen the inward corruption that has remained untouched within. He abhors himself. He is about as low as he can get — in dust and ashes — but he is now ready to be entrusted with twice what he had possessed before.

This is a wonderful test for us to put to our own hearts. Of whom do we speak the most — ourselves, mere mites in the great aggregate of humanity even though we have been redeemed, or do we speak largely of the Infinite God of immeasurable beauty and permanency? Our only safety lies in doing His will, for in doing His will the imperfect motivations of our own will are set aside in preference to His. In our speaking, the only speech that is safe is when we speak of Him. "He that seeketh his glory that sent him, the same is true, and no unrighteousness is in Him."

Andrew Murray says, "We want to get possession of the power, and use it; God wants the power to get possession of us and use us. If we give ourselves to the power to rule in us, the power will give itself to us to rule through us." — Lillian Harvey.

Nuts and Bolts

And those members of the body, which we think to be less honourable, upon these we bestow more abundant honour; and our uncomely parts have more abundant comeliness. For our comely parts have no need: but God hath tempered the body together, having given more abundant honour to that part which lacked (1 Cor. 12:23,24).

I WAS present at a board-meeting of a religious group, when controversy crept in. One member suddenly said, "There are too many chiefs, and not enough Injuns." It was only too true, for the desire of man is to procure prominence and status.

During World War II, an announcement came over the British radio that it took forty men on the ground to keep one pilot in the air. In religious groups, the tendency in every novice is the latent desire to be a pilot in the pulpit rather than be a faithful ground crewman.

L. E. Maxwell, founder of Prairie Bible Institute, must have encountered the same human trait in students for he said: "An interesting item in *Newsweek,* relates how U. S. President Johnson is finding it difficult to get career diplomats to accept important 'nuts and bolts' jobs within the State Department. Professional men, it is stated, prefer the more glamorous life of representing the U. S. abroad. But without the 'nuts and bolts' the State Department cannot long operate.

"God, too, needs 'nuts and bolts' workers! There are all kinds of jobs in the Kingdom of Heaven that need humble men and women to perform them. There is neither glamor nor glory attached to such jobs, but they must be done. Paul teaches in l Cor. 12 that each member of the Body of Christ is needed in order that the Body may efficiently function. No individual can deny his place in the divine program.

"In mission societies, 'nuts and bolts' workers are desperately needed. These missionaries need to accept their place and position and get on with the job. The job will never be done if men and women are looking for positions of prestige and power. Christ Himself taught that he who would be greatest in the kingdom must become the servant of all. Are you a 'nut and bolt' worker? Then keep at your task. Do not become discouraged. Yours is a vital ministry."

"If you're too big," someone has said, "to willingly do little things, you are probably too little to be trusted with big things." John Harrison at twenty-one had gone out to Africa with C. T. Studd, with a fiery enthusiasm to preach Christ. He watched his mates being sent out one by one to oversee surrounding districts, and when he asked to be sent out too, Studd replied with a decisive "No." Instead, he was given the job of sharpening scissors. Although resentment filled his heart, he did the task well, and all the tools of the mission station were brought to him for repair. He fully intended to tell Mr. Studd that he had not come to Africa to do odd jobs but to preach, but God spoke through Romans 6,7,8 and there under "the illumination of the Spirit" he came to see and take his true position, as crucified with Christ, and to give Christ the throne of his heart.

For nine years, he was faithful at typing, listening in on native palavers, mending broken things, repairing shoes, etc. At the death of Mr. Studd, Harri, as he was called, was the chosen successor. He had been trained in little things. He would be faithful in much. — Lillian Harvey.

It is natural for us to think if we could do some great exploit, or carry through some great piece of self-denial, we should be high in the kingdom. But it is not so. It is doing something that nobody sees but the Master Himself, and no one knows but He. — Andrew Bonar.

If the prophet had bid thee do some great thing, wouldest thou not have done it? how much rather then, when he saith to thee, Wash, and be clean? (2 Kings 5:13).

Greatness in Disguise

He was in the world . . . and the world knew him not. He came unto his own, and his own received him not (John 1:10,11).
He was before me. And I knew him not (John 1:30,31).

BISHOP Roberts, on returning from a general conference, applied to a Methodist family to whom he had been recommended. He was, as usual, humble in dress, dusty and weary. The family, taking him to be a rustic traveler, permitted him to put up and feed his horse and take his seat in the living-room. Supper was over, and no one inquired if he had eaten on the way.

The preacher of the circuit was stopping at the same house. He was young and frivolous and spent the evening in gay conversation with the daughter of the family, alluding occasionally and contemptuously to the "old man" who sat silently in the corner.

The good Bishop, after sitting a long time, with no other attention than these allusions, retired to bed. The bedroom was over the sitting-room, and, while praying with fatherly feeling for the faithless young preacher, he still heard the gay jesting and rude laughter. At last, the family retired without devotions. The young preacher slept in the same room with the Bishop. "Well, old man," said he as he got into bed, "Are you not asleep yet?"

"I am not, sir," replied the Bishop.

"Where have you come from?"

"From east of the mountains."

"From east of the mountains? What place?"

"Baltimore, sir."

"Baltimore—the seat of our general conference. Did you hear anything about it? We expect Bishop Roberts to stop here on his way home."

"Yes, sir," replied the Bishop humbly. "It ended before I left."

"Did you ever see Bishop Roberts?"

"Yes, sir, often; we left Baltimore together."

"You left Baltimore together? What's your name, my friend?"

"Roberts, sir."

"Roberts! Roberts! Excuse me, sir, but are you related to the Bishop?"

"They usually call me Bishop Roberts, sir."

"Bishop Roberts! Bishop Roberts! Are you Bishop Roberts, sir?" exclaimed the agitated young man. Embarrassed, he implored the good man's pardon, insisted on calling up the family, and seemed willing to do anything to redeem himself. The Bishop gave him an affectionate admonition, which he promised with tears never to forget. The venerable and compassionate man knew the frivolity of youth. He gave the young preacher much parental advice and prayed with him, but would not allow the family to be called, though he had eaten nothing since breakfast.

The next morning, after praying again with the young man, he left before the family had risen that he might save them a mortifying explanation. At the next conference, the renewed, young itinerant called upon the Bishop; weeping, he acknowledged his error and became a useful minister. Bishop Roberts often alluded to the incident, but would never tell the name of the young preacher. — Unknown.

> Greatness consists not in such empty gauds
> As dazzle and attract the public eye;
> It rests not on the breath of multitudes,
> For soothly hath the poet said: "The world
> Knows nothing of its greatest men." There went
> A great man once about the daily paths
> Of life, and few there were that recognized
> The greatness that in goodness dwelt;
> And still small is the number unto whom this truth
> Is made apparent.
> — Unknown.

He Made Himself of No Reputation

Let this mind be in you, which was also in Christ Jesus: Who . . . made himself of no reputation, and took upon him the form of a servant, and was made in the likeness of men (Phil. 2:5,7).

A WEALTHY young woman, daughter of a Prussian mine-owner, was apprehended by God for a specific mission. Leaving the comforts of her father's castle, she stooped to the lowly, the sick, and the needy all about her and disdained the honors of court society. Eva von Winkler, known as Sister Eva, not only took the lowly station herself but, like Francis of Assisi, inspired hundreds of others to join her in her labor among the destitute. She explains the reason for her thus stooping in one of her writings:

"Christ emptied Himself. He divested Himself of the royal insignia of the glory of God and even after He had left the Heavenly glory, denied Himself the permissible possessions and pleasures of this earth.

"Covetousness and self-emptying stand as contrasts in the history of humanity and salvation. Covetousness is the principle and motive power that governs the actions of the first Adam, as self-emptying is of the Second. The first Adam coveted to be like God, to have and to possess, to enjoy, to dominate and govern himself and everything within reach. Do we recognize ourselves in this picture? Self-denial, renouncement, giving up, giving and sharing to the uttermost self-surrender that does not withhold the very lifeblood — that is the life-principle of the second Adam, the Founder of a new human race, redeemed from self and from all selfish desire. To which line do we belong?

"Do the laws of life of the old Adam rule us with their selfish greed, or has the mind of Christ taken possession of us so that, constrained by His love, we no longer live unto ourselves? The dark stable and the lowly manger preach us a moving sermon on how utterly love can humble and empty itself. The rejoicing of the heavenly world over this, God's revelation of the willing sacrifice of Love, provides a strange contrast with the poor and painful circumstances in which Christ was born. The angels' rejoicing song accompanied the laying aside of the majesty and light of the glory of the Godhead.

"I wonder, do the holy angels weep when they see the redeemed children of God seeking honor, esteem, comfort, wealth, the pleasures of this life, and earthly happiness?"

> That glorious Form, that Light unsufferable,
>   And that far-beaming blaze of Majesty
> Wherewith He wont at Heaven's high council-table
>   To sit the midst of Trinal unity,
>   He laid aside; and here with us to be,
>   Forsook the courts of everlasting day
>   And chose with us a darksome house of mortal clay.
>   — John Milton in
>   "On the Morning of Christ's Nativity."

Be humble, as He also was humble. Though existing before the worlds in the Eternal Godhead, yet He did not cling with avidity to the prerogatives of His divine majesty, did not ambitiously display His equality with God; but divested Himself of the glories of Heaven, and took upon Him the nature of a servant, assuming the likeness of men. Nor was this all. Having thus appeared among men in the fashion of man, He humbled Himself yet more, and carried out His obedience even to dying. Nor did He die by a common death; He was crucified, as the lowest malefactor is crucified. . . .

It was a death which involved not intense suffering only but intense shame also: a death on which the Mosaic law has uttered a curse (Deut. 21:23), and which even Gentiles consider the most foul and most cruel of punishments; which has been ever after to the Jews a stumbling-block and to the Greeks foolishness. — Bishop Lightfoot.

Take Off the Fancy Dress

But woe unto you, scribes and Pharisees, hypocrites! for ye shut up the kingdom of heaven against men: for ye neither go in yourselves, neither suffer ye them that are entering to go in (Matt. 23:13).

IT is a terrible thing that the worst of all the vices can smuggle itself into the very center of our religious life. But you can see why. The other and less bad vices come from the devil working on us through our animal nature. But this does not come through our animal nature at all. It comes direct from Hell. It is purely spiritual: consequently, it is far more subtle and deadly. For the same reason, Pride can often be used to beat down the simpler vices. Teachers, in fact, often appeal to a boy's Pride, or, as they call it, his self-respect, to make him behave decently: many a man has overcome cowardice, or lust, or ill-temper by learning to think that they are beneath his dignity — that is, by Pride.

The devil laughs. He is perfectly content to see you becoming chaste and brave and self-controlled provided all the time, he is setting up in you the Dictatorship of Pride — just as he would be quite content to see your chilblains cured if he was allowed in return, to give you cancer. For Pride is spiritual cancer: it eats up the very possibility of love, or contentment, or even common-sense. . . .

We must not think Pride is something God forbids because He is offended at it, or that Humility is something He demands as due to His own dignity — as if God Himself was proud. He is not in the least worried about His dignity. The point is, He wants you to know Him: wants to give you Himself. And He and you are two things of such a kind that if you really get into any kind of touch with Him you will, in fact, be humble — delightedly humble — feeling the infinite relief of having for once got rid of all the silly nonsense about your own dignity which has made you restless and unhappy all your life. He is trying to make you humble in order to make this moment possible: trying to take off a lot of silly, ugly, fancy-dress in which we have all got ourselves up and are strutting about like the little idiots we are.

I wish I had got a bit further with humility myself: if I had, I could probably tell you more about the relief, the comfort, of taking the fancy-dress off — getting rid of the false self, with all its "look at me" and "aren't I a good boy?" and all its posing and posturing. To get even near it even for a moment is like a drink of cold water to a man in a desert.

Do not imagine that if you meet a really humble man he will be what most people call "humble" nowadays: he will not be a sort of greasy, smarmy person, who is always telling you that, of course, he is nobody. Probably all you will think about him is that he seemed a cheerful, intelligent chap who took a real interest in what you said to him. If you do dislike him it will be because you feel a little envious of anyone who seems to enjoy life so easily. He will not be thinking about humility: he will not be thinking about himself at all.

If anyone would like to acquire humility, I can, I think, tell him the first step. The first step is to realize that one is proud. And a biggish step too. At least, nothing whatever can be done before it. If you think you are not conceited, it means you are very conceited indeed. — C. S. Lewis in *Mere Christianity*. Used by kind permission of Harper/Collins.

And the devil did grin
For his darling sin,
   Is pride that apes humility.
          — Coleridge.

An old lady (after hearing the parable of the publican and the Pharisee) said, "Dear God, I thank Thee that I am not like that horrible Pharisee."

A Little Push Downward

To this man will I look, even to him that is poor and of a contrite spirit, and trembleth at my word (Isa. 66:2).

AN amusing story was told in the *Christian Herald* quite a number of years ago of a Dr. Hoffman who was converted but could not find the peace of mind he had so desired. "One day he asked a minister what the matter was with his spiritual life. The latter was, unfortunately, unable to help him. After that, Dr. Hoffman met a Salvation Army lady worker, to whom he told what had happened, and asked her to give him a little push upwards. 'Doctor,' she said, 'Are you sure you want a push upwards? Do you not think it is a little push downward that you require?' And immediately he felt convinced that she was right. He still had some dark days in his life, but ever found the thought of a 'little push downward' would always bring relief."

I used to think that God's gifts were on shelves one above the other, and that the taller we grew in Christian character the easier we could reach them. I now find that God's gifts are on shelves one beneath the other, and that it is not a question of growing taller, but of stooping lower, and that we have to go down, always down, to get His best gifts. —F. B. Meyer.

It has been deemed a great paradox in Christianity that it makes humility the avenue to glory. Yet what other avenue is there to wisdom or even to knowledge? Would you pick up precious truths, you must bend down and look for them. Everywhere the pearl of great price lies bedded in a shell which has no form or comeliness. It is so in physical science. Bacon has declared it: *natura non nisi parendo vincitur,* and the triumphs of science since his days have proved how willing nature is to be conquered by those who will obey her. It is so in moral speculation. Wordsworth has told us the law of his own mind, the fulfillment of which has enabled him to reveal a new world of poetry: "Wisdom is oft times nearer when we stoop than when we soar." — Unknown.

> He that is down needs fear no fall;
> He that is low no pride;
> He that is humble, ever shall
> Have God to be his guide.
> — John Bunyan.

Humiliation of soul always brings a positive blessing with it. If we empty our hearts of self, God will fill them with His love. He who desires a close communion with Christ should remember the word of the Lord, "To this man will I look, even to him that is poor and of a contrite spirit, and trembleth at my word." Stoop if you would climb to Heaven. Do we not say of Jesus, "He descended that He might ascend?" So must you. You must grow downwards, that you may grow upwards, for the sweetest fellowship with Heaven is to be had by humble souls, and by them alone. God will deny no blessing to a thoroughly humbled spirit. — C.H. Spurgeon.

Do you wish to be great? Then begin by being little. . . . Think first about the foundations of humility. The higher your structure is to be, the deeper must be its foundation. Modest humility is beauty's crown. — Unknown.

The tree grows best skyward that grows most downward; the lower the saint grows in humility, the higher he grows in holiness. — Unknown.

An epitaph on Hooker's monument by William Cowper reads:
> "He that lay so long obscurely low,
> Doth now preferred to greater honors go.
> Ambitious men, learn hence to be more wise,
> Humility is the true way to rise:
> And God in me this lesson did inspire,
> To bid this humble man, 'Friend, sit up higher.'"

Cease Striving to be Great

When thou wast little in thine own sight, wast thou not made the head of the tribes of Israel, and the Lord anointed thee king over Israel? (1 Sam. 15:17).

EDWARD Payson, who labored as a Congregational minister in New England for many years, told of a discovery he made which altered his whole outlook and gave him rest and happiness:

"I took up a little book in which various persons related their own experiences. Two of them agreed in remarking that they were never happy until they ceased striving to be great men. This remark struck me, as you know the most simple remarks will strike us when Heaven pleases. It occurred to me at once that most of my sins and sufferings were occasioned by an unwillingness to be the nothing which I am, and by consequent struggles to be something. I saw that if I would but cease struggling and consent to be anything or nothing, just as God pleases, I might be happy.

"You will think it strange that I mention this as a new discovery. In one sense it was not new; I had known it for years. But I now saw it in a new light. My heart saw it and consented to it. And I am comparatively happy.

"My dear brother, if you can give up all desire to be great and feel heartily willing to be nothing, you will be happy too. You must not even wish to be a great Christian; that is, you must not wish to make great attainments in religion for the sake of knowing that you have made them, or for the sake of having others think that you have made them.

"'Very good, very true,' you will say, 'though somewhat trite. But how am I to bring myself to such a state?'

"Let me ask in reply, 'Why are you not troubled when you see one man receive military and another Masonic honors? Why are you not unhappy because you cannot be a colonel, a general, or a most worshipful grand high priest?'

"'Because,' you answer, 'I have no desire for these titles or distinctions.'

"And why do you not desire them? Simply because you are not running a race of competition with those who obtain them. You stand aside and say, 'Let those who wish for these things, have them.'

"Now if you can, in a similar manner, give up all competition with respect to other objects—if you can stand aside from the race which too many other ministers are running and say, from your heart, 'Let those who choose to engage in such a race divide the prize; let one minister run away with the money, and another with the esteem, and a third with the applause; I have something else to do, a different race to run; be God's approbation the only prize for which I run; let me obtain that, and it is enough' —I say if you can, from the heart, adopt this language, you will find most of your difficulties and sufferings vanish.

"But it is hard to say this. It is almost impossible to persuade any man to renounce the race without cutting off his feet or, at least, fettering him.

"This God has done for me; this He has been doing for you. And you will one day, if you do not now, bless Him for all your sufferings, as I do for mine. I have not suffered one pang too much. God was never more kind than when I thought Him most unkind; never more faithful than when I was ready to say, 'His faithfulness has failed'.... Anything is a blessing that prevents us from running the fatal race which we are so prone to run, which first convinces us that we are nothing and then makes us will to be so."

Be not ashamed, my brother, to stand before the proud and powerful
With your white robes of simpleness.
Let your crown be of humility, your freedom the freedom of the soul;
Build God's throne daily upon the ample barrenness of your poverty,
And know that which is huge is not great, and pride is not everlasting. —Rabindranath Tagore.

The Venom of Pride

O Lucifer . . . thou hast said in thine heart, I will ascend into heaven, I will exalt my throne above the stars of God. . . . I will ascend above the heights of the clouds; I will be like the most High (Isa. 14:12-14).

PRIDE is a natural trait in man; humility comes only with grace from God. We here quote John Wesley: "In all the copious language of the Greeks there was not one word for humility till it was made by the great Apostle Paul. The whole Roman language, even with all the improvements of the Augustan age, does not afford so much as a name for humility."

Humility is a word which owes all its loveliness to Christianity; in Latin it is a term of contempt and means abjectness! The Greek word was regarded as a synonym of poor-spirited baseness. St. Peter, thinking how Christ girded Himself with a towel and washed the disciples' feet, bids Christians tie humble-mindedness round them with knots like a slave's apron. *Humanitas* meant in Latin "human nature" or "refined culture." In Christian language it means love to the whole brotherhood of man. Well may the author of the Epistle to Diognetus say, "What the soul is to the body, that Christianity is to the world." — Dean Farrar.

There never was a saint yet that grew proud of his fine feathers, but what the Lord plucked them out by and by. There never yet was an angel that had pride in his heart, but he lost his wings and fell in Gehenna, as Satan and those fallen angels did. And there never shall be a saint who indulges self-conceit and pride and self-confidence, but the Lord will spoil his glories and trample his honors in the mire. — C.H. Spurgeon.

O hateful Pride! What ruin hast thou caused
E'er since thou first drew'st breath, aye, poisoned breath
In an archangel's mind; and there didst brood
So sullenly, and germinated sin,
Which found expression in that overt act
Of proud rebellion 'gainst the sovereign sway
Of God, the King of kings: thus Lucifer,
By thee impelled, O Pride, incurred God's wrath,
Was hurled from Heaven headlong to those dark shades
Of hell, together with his rebel band.

So, cast from Heaven, thou roamest through the earth
Instilling in men's minds thy venomed spawn,
Sometimes appearing open to the view,
At other times so wrapped in specious guise
That thou dost pass 'mongst mortals unobserved.
Beneath the somber garb of monk or nun
Or dress of Quaker-like simplicity
Beat hearts — aye, just as proud as fashion's slaves
For these are but puffed up with finery —
The others proud of their humility. . . .
The preacher too, O Pride, is dogg'd by thee,
And he — unless the grace of God prevent —
Will seek his own renown, and court the smiles,
Or shun the frowns, of hearers in the pews.

And yet, O Pride, thou wast on earth o'ercome
By Christ, the Righteous One! By Him alone;
When Thy most cunning shafts in vain were spent,
And all thy blandishments unheeded fell.
'Twas He forsook the radiant realms of bliss
And veiled His Deity in human flesh
To take a lowly place amongst the men —
His creatures — who had scorned Him: yea, He died!
And thus He wrought His vast salvation plan
To bring in full redemption for His Bride —
His own loved Church: and now on them no more
Canst thou, base Pride, assert Thy fatal sway
Although to tempt thou still art always prone:
But soon thy weapons shall, all broken, fall,
And thou be banished to thy pending doom. . . .
                                                    — Unknown.

Ridiculous Conceit

Talk no more so exceeding proudly; let not arrogancy come out of your mouth: for the Lord is a God of knowledge, and by him actions are weighed (1 Sam. 2:3).
Pride and arrogancy . . . do I hate. (Prov. 8:13).

SOME are of the opinion that intellectual attainments make men proud, but long experience with students and applicants for religious work has convinced me that it is often the ignorant and those most lacking in talent and ability who give the most trouble. They are not aware of how little they have attained. Often they do not reveal why they are peeved or hurt, but eventually it comes out that they thought they ought to be occupying a position for which they had the fewest of talents and the least of knowledge.

It was the man with the fewest talents who had the grievance against his master and hid what he had in the earth. He had not even enough common sense to put the money out to usury so that the interest accrued could be returned to his lord. In psychiatric wards, where the occupants are no longer aware of how foolish their pride truly is, you can find those who believe they are Queen Elizabeth, Napoleon, or some great preacher. Oh how ridiculous pride makes a man or woman who has not bared his heart before God and gotten a true estimate of his own powers! —Lillian Harvey.

"And this," said the German guide, pointing to an old-fashioned instrument, "is Beethoven's piano, the very one on which he composed many of his most famous works."

A party of tourists was being conducted round the musician's home at Bonn. One relic after another had been viewed, and now they were being shown the greatest treasure of all. "Did Beethoven really play this instrument?" asked a girl, rather disdainfully. Obviously her opinion of the old piano was not very high.

"He did," replied the guide. "It is one of our priceless possessions." Plainly he reverenced the name of Beethoven for his eyes lit up when he spoke of the great composer.

The light died suddenly, however, as the girl who had asked the question sat down at the piano and began playing a popular foxtrot. Turning from the instrument, she said lightly, "I suppose you get lots of tourists playing this piano?"

"We certainly get many visitors," replied the guide coldly. "Only last year I had the honor of conducting the great Paderewski through these rooms."

"And did he play the piano?"

"No. He considered himself unworthy even to lay a finger on it." —H. L. Gee in *Joyful News*.

A top-ranking British official in the Orient entertained a sophisticated lady as his guest. It seems that the general's assistant had seated this lady at the left hand of her host rather than in the place of honor at the right. Having borne the matter as long as she could, the lady burst out, "I suppose you have great difficulty getting your aide-de-camp to seat your guests properly at the table."

"Oh, not at all,' replied the general. "Those who matter don't mind, and those who mind don't matter. . . ."

—*The Evangel.*

Conceit is the compensation of benignant nature for mental deficiency. —Unknown.

> Pride transformed Eden into Hell
> Where demons unforbidden dwell;
> With poisoned breath it smothers life
> And with one finger stirs up strife.
> It alienates the soul from God
> And slowly starves it of its food. . . .
> —Trudy Tait.

Self-Reliance is God-Defiance

Six things doth the LORD hate: yea, seven are an abomination unto him:
A proud look . . . (Prov. 6:16, 17).
Him that hath an high look and a proud heart will not I suffer (Psa. 101:5).

SELF-RELIANCE is God-defiance," said Geoffrey Bull, a former missionary who was held under Communist arrest.

William Law in his book, *Serious Call*, reiterated that same truth over two hundred years ago: "It (pride) has the guilt of stealing as it gives to ourselves those things which belong only to God; and it has the guilt of lying, as it is the denying the truth of our state, and pretending to be something that we are not.

". . . Pride can degrade the highest angels into devils, and humility raise fallen flesh and blood to the thrones of angels. . . . Pride must die in you, or nothing of Heaven can live in you. Under the banner of the truth, give yourself up to the meek and humble Spirit of the holy Jesus.

"Humility must sow the seed, or there can be no reaping in Heaven. Look not at pride only as an unbecoming temper, nor at humility only as a decent virtue, for the one is death, and the other is life; the one is all hell, the other is all heaven. So much as you have of pride within you, you have of the fallen angel alive in you; so much as you have of true humility, so much you have of the Lamb of God within you.

"Could you see what every stirring of pride does to your soul, you would beg of everything you meet to tear the viper from you though with the loss of a hand or an eye. Could you see what a sweet, divine, transforming power there is in humility, how it expels the poison of your nature, and makes room for the Spirit of God to live in you, you would rather wish to be the footstool of all the world than want the smallest degree of it. . . .

"That humility which is despised by men now, and is so contrary to the spirit of this world, will overcome the world, the flesh, and the devil. He who dares to be poor and contemptible in the eyes of this present evil world in order to approve himself to God — who resists and rejects all human glory; who opposes the clamor of his passions, meekly bears all injuries and wrongs, and dares to wait for his reward until the invisible hand of God gives to every one his proper place — that one will be found to be the man of true wisdom in the coming day. He is the good soldier of Jesus Christ who has fought the good fight of faith. Yet it cannot have been in his own strength or wisdom but only as he has embraced the death of Christ as the crucifixion of his own devilish self, and through the power of the Holy Spirit has known the indwelling life of the meek and lowly Lamb of God in his soul."

My faith looks up to claim that touch divine
Which robs me of this fatal strength of mine,
And leaves me resting wholly, Lord, on Thine.

Yes, make me such a one as Thou canst bless,
Meet for Thy use through very helplessness;
Thine, only Thine, the glory of success.

Lord, teach Thy trembling saints to find like Thee
The place of death, the place of victory,
Like Thee, to triumph in extremity.

For still Thy cross shall be our conquering sign;
Then first we live when we our lives resign,
Yes, all our being is the being Thine.
— Unknown.

If we be sitting at the feet of Jesus, all carnal boasting is excluded; we have His mind of wisdom in all things, and cannot behave ourselves unseemly. — R. C. Chapman.

Exalting Our Gate

He that exalteth his gate seeketh destruction (Prov. 17:19).

IN the lawless East, houses and churches exposed to the attacks of robbers have low doorways, so that you have almost to stoop to enter them. The Bedouins of the desert are splendid riders, and go on their plundering expeditions always on horseback. They would consider it beneath their dignity to attack any place on foot. And hence, they make raids only on horseback. The houses of the rich and the noble in the East have courts like the palaces of Italy, into which you can drive in a carriage from the street. It is only such houses that are worth entering, for it is only in such houses that sufficient plunder can be got to repay the risk. . . .

Now, what the wise man means by his proverb is, that if you are proud and haughty, you will expose yourself to dangers as great in your life as the man exposes himself to who exalts the gate of his house, and so invites the Bedouin robber to enter in on horseback and murder him or plunder his goods.

There are foes as deadly and possessed of powers of mischief as great as the Bedouin robbers, who are ready to take advantage of the opening you give them by cherishing an arrogant and lofty spirit, to enter into your hearts and rob you of all that is dearest and most precious in your life.

There are many sins that, like Spanish beggars, ride only upon horseback; vices that carry things with a high hand, that assume lofty airs and make themselves big and consequential. They never dismount; they never enter your heart on foot. As if knowing how puny and weak-kneed they really are, they must impose upon the imagination, and raise themselves on high by outward circumstances. You hear it said of a man in a proud and haughty mood, "He is on his high horse."

Now, to admit these proud, lofty sins that ride on horseback as it were, you must lift high the gate of your heart. They cannot cross the threshold of a lowly mind; and if you do not exalt your gate, these high-flying sins will not trouble you; you are beneath their consideration. You are too low for pride, and scorn, and worldly ambition, and high-mindedness to enter in; but thank God not too low for the Kingdom of Heaven which stoops to the lowest, which belongs of right to the poor in spirit, to creep through and fill and sanctify your heart. From the proverb of the text, therefore, you learn the wisdom of stooping.

The celebrated Benjamin Franklin of America, who was the first to draw down the lightnings of heaven to the earth by means of a child's kite, was once, when a young man, shown out of the house of a friend he had been visiting by a narrow passage. As he was going along it his friend hurriedly said, "Stoop, stoop!" Not understanding the advice, Franklin struck his head violently against a beam that projected overhead. "My lad," said his friend, "you are young, and the world is before you; learn to stoop as you go through it, and you will save yourself many a hard blow.". . .

If you exalt your gate, you court the coming into your heart of pride and fury, which will rob you of your reason, and make you say and do foolish things in your haste. Lower your gate, then, that only the quiet, meek grace of humility and gentleness can come in. — Hugh Macmillan.

> Humble we must be if to Heaven we go;
> High is the roof there, but the gate is low.
> — Robert Herrick.

> If that in sight of God is great
> Which counts itself for small,
> We by that law humility
> The chiefest grace must call;
> Which being such, not knows itself
> To be a grace at all.
> — R. C. Trench.

The Low Door of the Cross

*I am the door: by me if any man enter in, he shall be saved (John 10:9).
. . . I am meek and lowly in heart: and ye shall find rest (Matt. 11:29).*

THE door of faith is a narrow one, for it lets no self-righteousness, no worldly glories, no dignities through. We are kept outside till we strip ourselves of crowns and royal robes, and stand clothed only in the hair-shirt of penitence. We must make ourselves small to get in. We must creep on our knees, so low is the vault; we must leave everything outside, so narrow is it. We must go in one by one. The door opens into a palace, but it is too strait for anyone who trusts to himself. — Alexander Maclaren.

Annie Johnson Flint entered into God's plan for her life through the narrow door of arthritis which, crippling her fingers, barred her from her anticipated career as a concert pianist. Although disappointed, she came to accept her wheel-chair existence. Through the poems which she gave to the world, her inner soul vibrated with grander music than any she could have played on the piano. The following is one of them:

> "Oh, strait and narrow is the door,
> The little door of loss,
> By which we enter in to Christ,
> The low door of the Cross:
> But when we put away our pride,
> And in contrition come,
> We find it is the only way
> That leads to God and Home.
>
> "Oh, strait and lowly are the doors
> By which Christ comes to us;

We bar the entrance gates of joy,
    And when He finds them thus,
By strange, small doors of woe and want,
    Of trial and of pain,
He enters in to share our lives
    To our eternal gain.

"The narrow doors He brings us to,
    The little doors and low,
What large rooms they will open on,
    If we will only go:
The strange, small doors of work and want,
    Strait doors of grief and pain,
What riches they will lead us to!
    What everlasting gain!"

Every soul who has found Christ has found Him through the low door of the cross. "I was exceedingly ambitious as a boy," said Samuel Logan Brengle, "to have a name that would ring around the world, that would set me on a pinnacle with everybody staring at me and acclaiming me, but when God sanctified me, I felt that the angels must look down upon the honors that men bestow upon each other about as we look down upon the honor that the ants in the anthill may bestow upon some distinguished ant-leader. It all looked so pitifully small to me and it does to this hour."

But Brengle was brought to that narrow door by a series of personal choices. He first stepped down from his anticipated career as a lawyer to be a preacher of God's glorious Gospel. Later, seeking the fullness of the Holy Spirit in his life, he stepped down from all ambition to be a "great" preacher who would influence his congregation by his glowing oratory, to the place of willingness to "stammer and stutter." He knew that his "honor and glory" would be reaped in Heaven.

The Door of Destitution

He will regard the prayer of the destitute, and not despise their prayer (Psa. 102:17).

"O LORD, drench us with humility," was the plea of Oswald Chambers, one of the most poignant and searching writers of the twentieth century. In one of his books, *He Shall Glorify Me,* he has much to say about this most needed attribute:

"Our Lord begins where we would never begin, at the point of human destitution. The greatest blessing a man ever gets from God is the realization that if he is going to enter into His Kingdom it must be through the door of destitution. Naturally we do not want to begin there, that is why the appeal of Jesus is of no use until we come face to face with realities; then the only One worth listening to is the Lord.

"We learn to welcome the patience of Jesus only when we get to the point of human destitution. It is not that God will not do anything for us until we get there, but that He cannot. God can do nothing for me if I am sufficient for myself. When we come to the place of destitution spiritually we find the Lord waiting, and saying, 'If any man thirst, let him come unto me and drink.' There are hundreds at the place of destitution and they don't know what they want. If I have been obeying the command of Jesus to 'go and make disciples' I know what they want; they want Him. We are so interested in our own spiritual riches that souls are white unto harvest all around us and we don't reap one for Him.

"Some men enter the Kingdom of Heaven through crushing, tragic, overwhelming conviction of sin, but they are not the greatest number; the greatest number enter the Kingdom along this line of spiritual destitution—no power to lay hold of God, no power to do what I ought to do, utterly poverty-stricken."

From a reading in *My Utmost for His Highest,* we add these few words on the same theme:

"The New Testament notices things which from our standards do not seem to count. 'Blessed are the poor in spirit,' literally—'Blessed are the paupers'—an exceedingly commonplace thing! The preaching of today is apt to emphasize strength of will, beauty of character—the things that are easily noticed. The phrase we hear so often, 'Decide for Christ,' is an emphasis on something our Lord never trusted. He never asks us to decide for Him, but to yield to Him, a very different thing. At the basis of Jesus Christ's Kingdom is the unaffected loveliness of the commonplace. The thing I am blessed in is my poverty. If I know I have no strength of will, no nobility of disposition, then Jesus says—'Blessed are you,' because it is through this poverty that I enter His Kingdom. I cannot enter His Kingdom as a good man or woman, I can only enter it as a complete pauper.

"The true character of the loveliness that tells for God is always unconscious. Conscious influence is priggish and un-Christian. If I say, 'I wonder if I am of any use,' I instantly lose the bloom of the touch of the Lord. 'He that believeth in me, out of him shall flow rivers of living water.' If I examine the outflow, I lose the touch of the Lord.

"Which are the people who have influenced us most? Not the ones who thought they did, but those who had not the remotest notion that they were influencing us. In the Christian life the implicit is never conscious; if it is conscious, it ceases to have this unaffected loveliness which is the characteristic of Jesus. We always know when Jesus is at work because He produces in the commonplace something that is inspiring."

Man's weakness waiting upon God, its end can never miss,
For man on earth no work can do more angel-like than this,
      To prove His strength.
            —Constance Ruspini.

Cherished Humblings

Thou shalt remember all the way which the Lord thy God led thee these forty years in the wilderness, to humble thee, and to prove thee, to know what was in thine heart, whether thou wouldest keep his commandments, or no. And he humbled thee (Deut. 8:2,3).

HELENA Garratt with two of her sisters left a comfortable home in beautiful surroundings to go out to Africa where they founded the African Evangelistic Band. In one of their periodicals she writes:

"There is a vast difference between what God thinks worthy of record and what we do. In recounting Israel's experiences, the Holy Ghost makes this record, 'He humbled thee.' We do not often find a Christian registering a like experience in his life story. Our minds seem to dwell more upon the rapturous moments in our past than on the humbling times. It seems to come more naturally to us to recount how God has used, or taught, or comforted us, than that He has humbled us.

"Perhaps some of us think that the humbling processes we have passed through are not worthy of record, and others of us feel that the slights, the losses, the disappointments we met with were so painful, so humiliating, that we would rather forget them. But it is the humblings that count with God, and He deems it worthy of eternal record that during the forty years of wilderness wandering, His people learned to be humble and to know themselves.

"As we draw nearer to God and better understand His ways, we learn to make records according to His mind. We begin to count His humiliations, His testings, His chastenings, as our most cherished spiritual experiences. The saint who has had the best year in God's sight is not the one who has had an easy path, or has achieved the highest success; not the one whose praises filled the lips of men, but the one who has known the deepest humblings in the presence of the Highest One, and who has bowed lowest at His feet. The Lord Jesus said, 'Whosoever shall humble himself . . . the same is greatest in the kingdom of heaven.'

"God did not tell His ancient people to remember only the battles fought and the enemies slain, but His Word was, 'Thou shalt remember all the way which the Lord thy God led thee . . . to humble thee and to prove thee.' His humblings are as divine as His upliftings; and it is His hand upon us, breaking us and emptying us, that makes us fit for His use.

"Let us not feel ashamed of the humiliating experiences, but rather glory in them. . . . Teach me to value and welcome all that Thou dost send me to humble me and to teach me dependence upon Thyself."

> His overthrow heaped happiness upon him;
> For then, and not till then, he felt himself,
> And found the blessedness of being little!
> —Shakespeare.

George MacDonald was great enough to record his humbling: "I learned that it is better, a thousandfold, for a proud man to fall and be humbled, than to hold up his head in his pride and fancied innocence. I learned that he that will be a hero, will barely be a man; that he that will be nothing but a doer of his work, is sure of his manhood. In nothing was my ideal lowered, or dimmed, or grown less precious; I only saw it too plainly to set myself for a moment beside it. Indeed, my ideal soon became my life; whereas, formerly, my life had consisted in a vain attempt to behold, if not my ideal in myself, at least myself in my ideal."

If I be content to be nothing, I cannot take offence; and when I am really humble and know myself a worm, I shall not complain if trampled on. —R. C. Chapman.

Disdaining Praise

But he is a Jew, which is one inwardly . . . whose praise is not of men, but of God (Rom. 2:29).
They loved the praise of men more than the praise of God (John 12:43).

THE test of a man of God is how he receives the plaudits of men. Henry Martyn, that noble missionary who expended his life for India, realized the danger of such praise when he said: "Men frequently admire me, and I am pleased, but I abhor the pleasure."

John Elliot, a Puritan settler in New England, became a missionary to the Indians. In a letter to the Honorable Robert Boyle on having been denominated "the Indian Evangelist," he wrote: "I do beseech you to suppress all such things. It is the Redeemer Who hath done what is done. I wish the word could be obliterated if any of the copies remain. Let me lie low!"

Later he wrote: "I am come to a conclusion to look for no great matters in the world, but to know Jesus Christ and Him crucified. I make best way in a low gale. A high spirit and a high sail together will be dangerous, and therefore I prepare to live low. I desire not much; I pray against it. My study is my calling, so much as to attend that without distraction. . . . By my secluded retirement I have advantages to observe how every day's occasions insensibly wear off the heart from God and bury it in itself, which they that ever live in the noise and lumber of the world cannot be sensible of."

How few archbishops there have been who would disdain honors and material benefits as did the humble Archbishop Leighton of the Church of England. He chose to live on only one-fifth of his income as archbishop and refused to accept the remainder. As a Bishop he also refused the title of "lord." This was not because he wished to affect humility, but because it was in his very nature to do so. When he wrote to a minister in a subordinate position he signed his name, "Your poor friend and servant."

The great physicist, Michael Faraday, once gave a lecture before an audience of London scientists. At the end the Prince of Wales arose to propose a vote of thanks. The motion was carried, but when they looked for the lecturer, he had disappeared through a back door on stage in order to attend a prayer meeting in the vicinity where he might renew his fellowship with God.

Isaac Newton, seeing the tremendous secrets which nature held in her bosom, said of himself that he felt like a lad walking along the shore, stooping to pick a few pebbles from the beach.

Samuel Logan Brengle disdained pulpit honors on more illustrious platforms to join himself with the then despised Salvation Army; eventually, however, he became a worldwide speaker. His wife wrote to him, "I think if all this hoisting up of our great men in front of the Cross could be stopped, it would be one great step toward regaining some of our lost power. Continue to insist on this in your case, and I believe God will greatly reward you.... I am sure it grieves God. You know I love to hear you lauded, and I can spend many happy hours at it. But when I go to meetings I want no one mentioned but the One Who can save people from sin." — Lillian Harvey.

> The Man Who was Lord of fate,
> Born in an ox's stall,
> Was great because He was much too great
> To care about greatness at all.
>
> You long to be great; you try;
> You feel yourself smaller still;
> In the name of God let ambition die;
> Let Him make you what He will.
> —George MacDonald.

Shun the Praise of Men

How can ye believe, which receive honour one of another, and seek not the honour that cometh from God only? (John 5:44).

"WHY then must your complaisance add fuel to a fire which I sometimes fear will burn up all my grace and my religion?" This was the reaction of the godly Philip Doddridge to a letter from an admirer who had highly lauded his literary attainments. He further bares his soul as he continues to refute the praise of this would-be well-wisher:

"Alas, such is your 'pious and excellent' friend! You compliment me on the learning and accuracy of my views. How are you deceived! I have hardly looked into many of the most excellent treatises of the ancient and modern commentators, and have only dipped into some others so far as to see that there was a great deal that I was not capable of comprehending, at least without a long course of preparatory study. There is hardly a chapter in the Bible which does not puzzle me, nor, in short, any considerable subject of human inquiry in which I do not perceive both my ignorance and my weakness. And this — is your oracle!

"I have this morning been humbling myself before God for the pride of my heart. It follows me whithersoever I go — into my study, into the conversation of my friends, and, what is most dreadful of all, into the immediate presence of my Maker; of that God Who is the Fountain of all perfection, and from Whose hands I have received my all, and from Whom I have deserved an aggravated condemnation.

"Such is the subtlety of this insinuating mischief, that I can recollect instances in which I have been proud of having exposed the deformity of pride with success, while perhaps it was only another instance of my degeneracy to imagine that I had so succeeded!

"How hard is it to keep self in self-subjection! This you have taught me as well as man can teach it, but God alone can make the excellent lesson effectual. I cannot lay a scheme for the honor of my God, and the service of the world, but self intrudes itself, and that sometimes to such a degree as to make me doubt whether the governing principle be not wrong, and whether many of my most valuable actions and designs be not *splendida pietata.*"

God gave unusual blessing to Philip Doddridge who knew how to shun the praise of men. His book, *The Rise and Progress of Religion in the Soul,* was used in the salvation of some very prominent men who in turn influenced multitudes. George Whitefield when reading it saw the way of salvation by faith and embraced it. William Wilberforce, traveling abroad with his Christian tutor, read this book and was so favorably impressed with the Gospel it proclaimed that he went on to study the New Testament which culminated in his new birth. Samuel Pearce, the Brainerd of the Baptists, also read it to his soul's good.

Philip Doddridge, the author of this book and other expositions on the Scriptures, was born on June 26, 1702. He ministered for twenty-one years in Northampton in a nonconformist church. Wishing to rivet his sermons home to his hearers, he would sometimes compose hymns for the occasion. "O Happy Day" is one such composition and an evidence of the happy change the Holy Spirit had wrought in his heart.

One great cause of our frequent conflict is that we have a secret desire to be rich, and it is the Lord's design to make us poor: we want to gain an ability of doing something, and He suits His dispensations to convince us that we can do nothing. We want a stock in ourselves, and He would have us absolutely dependent upon Him. So far as we are content to be weak that His power may be magnified in us, so far shall we make our enemies know that we are strong, though we ourselves shall never be directly sensible that we are so. Only by comparing what we are with the opposition we stand against, we may come to a comfortable conclusion that the Lord worketh mightily in us (Psa. 41:11). —John Newton.

Dangerous Flattery

A man that flattereth his neighbour spreadeth a net for his feet (Prov. 29:5).
A flattering mouth worketh ruin (Prov. 26:28).

A TRANSLATION of a certain book was sent to J. N. Darby by its author. In the preface, the writer had given a most flattering opinion of the eminence and piety of J. N. Darby. We give, in abbreviated form, the letter Darby sent to the author in which he repudiated the undue praise:

"Pride is the greatest of all evils that beset us, and of all our enemies it is that which dies the slowest and hardest; even the children of the world are able to discern this. Madam de Stael said on her deathbed, 'Do you know what is the last to die in man? It is "self-love."'

"God hates pride above all things because it gives to man the place that belongs to Him Who is above, exalted over all. Pride intercepts communion with God, and draws down His chastisement, for 'God resisteth the proud.'

"I am sure, then, you will feel, my dear friend, that one cannot do another a greater injury than by praising him and feeding his pride. 'A man that flattereth his neighbour spreadeth a net for his feet.' 'A flattering mouth worketh ruin.' Be assured, moreover, that we are too shortsighted to be able to judge of the degree of our brother's piety; we are not able to judge it aright without the balance of the sanctuary, and that is in the hand of Him Who searches the heart. Judge nothing, therefore, before the time, until the Lord come, and make manifest the counsels of the heart and render to every man his praise."

Barclay Buxton, who came of noble Quaker ancestry, was a godly missionary who founded the Japan Evangelistic Band. He realized, however, the dangers of praise. In his biography, his son has this to say on the subject: "Soon after his marriage, he asked my mother to keep from him any praise that she might hear concerning him or his addresses 'because pride is such a danger to me,' yet he rarely spoke of himself as proud men incessantly do."

Once when Hudson Taylor, the Founder of the China Inland Mission, was to speak, he was introduced as "our illustrious guest." Mr. Taylor stood quietly for a minute and then said, "I am the little servant of an illustrious Master."

J. D. Drysdale, a man widely known in the North of England for his excellent service for God, would often pray: "Lord, never permit me to enter the ministry until nonapparent success will not cause discouragement; or apparent success cause inflation and pride."

Service for the Master that everybody praises is very dangerous service. Perhaps in the day the Master returns, the name of one we never heard of in the Church of Christ may be the highest, because he did most, simply for the Master. — Andrew Bonar.

> Then learn to scorn the praise of men,
>   And learn to lose with God;
> For Jesus won the world through shame,
>   And beckons thee His road.
>
> God's glory is a wondrous thing,
>   Most strange in all its ways,
> And, of all things on earth, least like
>   What men agree to praise.
>
> As He can endless glory weave
>   From what men reckon shame,
> In His own world He is content
>   To play a losing game.
>   — Frederick Faber.

Return it to God

There are not found that returned to give glory to God, save this stranger (Luke 17:18).

AN extremely talented concert pianist, composer, and gifted piano teacher, gave her students her recipe for keeping a humble spirit. "When people compliment me," she said, "instead of feeding on their praise so that it makes me proud, I put it all in a little basket and at the end of the day I kneel down and offer the basket to Him. 'Here, Lord, it's all Yours,' I tell Him. 'It doesn't belong to me. I give it back to You.'"

John Wesley, the founder of Methodism, reveals the secret of the unusual favor God bestowed upon him over a period of fifty years in the prayer quoted below. He passed the prayer on to his much admired colleague, John Fletcher, the Vicar of Madeley. Fletcher passed it on to another friend with these words: "When you have done anything for God or received any favor from Him, retire, if not into your closet, into your heart and say:

"'I come, Lord, to restore to Thee what Thou hast given and I freely relinquish it, to enter again into nothingness. For what is the most perfect creature in Heaven or earth in Thy presence but a void, capable of being filled with Thee and by Thee, as the air which is void and dark is capable of being filled with the light of the sun? Grant therefore, O Lord, that I may never appropriate Thy grace to myself any more than the air appropriates to itself the light of the sun, who withdraws it every day to restore it the next, there being nothing in the air that either appropriates his light or resists it. Oh, give me the same facility of receiving and restoring Thy grace and good works! I say, "Thine"; for I acknowledge that the root from which they spring is in Thee and not in me.'"

John Fletcher adds: "The true means to be filled anew with the riches of His grace is thus to strip ourselves of it;

89

without this, it is extremely difficult not to faint in the practice of good works. Therefore, that your good works may receive their last perfection, let them lose themselves in God. This is a kind of death to them, resembling that of our bodies, which will not attain their highest life, their immortality, till they lose themselves in the glory of our souls, or rather of God, wherewith they shall be filled. And it is only what they had of earthly and mortal which good works lose by this spiritual death."

Christ specially noted the one leper who had returned to give thanks, for He loves us to acknowledge that all comes from Him. Not until the soul is given up fully to God, does it feel that spontaneous uprising of thankfulness to Him for the smallest benefits. "Never did I feel true gratitude in my heart," said a young woman, "until I had yielded myself up fully to God to either live or die for Him. The Holy Spirit then took the throne of my heart and only then it was that upon retiring to bed, for the first time, I thanked Him for the lovely bed upon which I had sought repose. I realized how ungrateful my heart had been all through those years of former halfhearted Christian living. Like the nine lepers, I had never returned to give thanks for the manifold blessings, both large and small, He had so graciously bestowed upon me."

> Why am I weak, when Thou art strong,
>   And I might draw my strength from Thee?
> Why am I poor, when Thou art rich,
>   Lord, Who hast bought all good for me?
>
> Hast Thou not taken on Thyself,
>   All insufficiency of mine?
> Then let me mine own self forget,
>   And take, and use each gift of Thine.
>
> O work out all Thy will in me!
>   My inmost being, Lord, control,
> That so my life may manifest
>   The risen Life, within my soul.
>   —E. H. Divall.

Not by Man's Might or Power

My speech and my preaching was not with enticing words of man's wisdom, but in demonstration of the Spirit and of power (1 Cor. 2:4).

THE young aspiring preacher had tried twenty-two churches as a probationer before he was accepted. It looked like failure, but in reality it was success. Marcus Dods was so assured of the power of truth that he would not embellish the divine message by his own eloquent or passionate pleas in the pulpit. His impassive and massive figure did not appeal to many of his shallow hearers who wished their young minister to rouse their dull spirits by animated gestures in the pulpit. But a man with a message is bound to eventually find a hearing. A Glasgow Church enjoyed his ministry for over twenty years. Then he filled a Chair in Edinburgh University where his influence was felt by many young men.

"He was the best friend and the most Christlike man I have ever known," said W. Robertson Nicoll of Marcus Dods. "He was the humblest of men, and he never offered counsel unless it was asked for. But unconsciously he had a haunting influence on those who knew him. Unconsciously he prompted them to do right." It takes great humility and faith to be different. But could a man who refused to comply with the popular demands for a minister ever succeed? We will let Professor Henry Drummond tell us the profound effect this man's message had upon his hearers:

"He stands squarely in the pulpit, without either visible motion or emotion, reads his sermon from start to finish, without a pause, begins without awakening any sense of expectation, gives no hint throughout of either discovery or originality, however much the discourse may seem to teem with both, passes at a pace which never changes, in a voice without passion or pathos, or cadence, or climax . . . and

91

finishes bluntly when the thing has been said, as if he were now well out of it for the week.

"But, on thinking over it when you get home, you perceive that the after result is almost in proportion to the unconsciousness of the effect at the time. You know exactly why the sermon stopped just then; there was nothing more to be said; the proof was final. You discover easily why the appeal did not move you more. You have been accustomed to the sound of passion, vibrating in the chords of another soul. Now your own soul seethes and trembles. These effects are not the work of man; they are the operating of the Spirit of Truth.

"You know at last why the man was so hidden, why he had no cunning phrases, why beautiful words do not linger in your memory, why a preacher so impersonal, and to whom you were so impersonal, a preacher so wholly uninterested in you, so innocent himself of taking you by the throat, has yet taken his subject by the throat and planted it down before your inmost being, so that you cannot get rid of it. You know that you have heard no brilliant or awakening oratory, but you feel that you have been searched and overawed, that unseen realities have looked you in the eyes and asked you questions and made you a more humble and a more obedient man."

"Slowly indeed, and unseen does His work proceed," said Marcus Dods in his commentary on Corinthians, "Slowly because the work is for eternity, and because only gradually can moral and spiritual evils be removed. 'It is by no breath, turn of eye, wave of hand, salvation joins issue with death,' but by actual and sustained moral conflict, by real sacrifice and persistent choice of good, by long trial and development of individual character, by the slow growth of nations and the interaction of social and religious influences, by the leavening of all that is human with the spirit of Christ, that is, with self-development by practical life to the good of men. All this is too great and too real to be other than slow."

Sink Your Own Cause in His

I laboured . . . yet not I, but the grace of God which was with me (1 Cor. 15:10).

MARCUS Dods reveals some of the secrets he learned by divine revelation in his book, *Footsteps in the Path of Life:*

"To be truly servants of God, this is the difficulty — to sink our own cause and prospects and will in the cause of God; to be truly in God's hand, to be used as He wills; to come back day by day and wait for orders from Him; to acquire thus the understanding of what He seeks to do in the world, and gradually to abjure every other thought than how to accomplish this, to be consecrated and to be faithful; this is what God requires of us all.

"To this God will bring you, so that the hopes and plans of merely selfish advancement are just so much affliction and sorrow sown for you; the eager ambitions that burn in your hearts and stimulate you to work are but driving you off the road, and from them all you must return to the simplicity of God's servants who care only to please Him. It is when we have no aim but this that we find rest.

"It matters little in what form our self-seeking shows itself. We strive to improve our character, and gradually it dawns on us that the reason our efforts are vain is that we are striving to do God's will, not simply because it is God's will, but because we shall be worthier persons if we do it — striving to live a new life with an old heart. Self is our center and object, and all is wrong with us till God is our object, till we truly, simply, and directly love Him."

In another reading by Dods entitled "The Monarchy Within Us," he writes:

"We are to bear in mind, that God also has a will; that as by our wills we plan and set ourselves resolutely in one direction,

93

so there are plans which have their origin in a will that is not of earth, but are yet to be carried out on earth; that alongside of our desires there are the things which God is desiring to be done.

"Everywhere, and in all things, we are to meet the will of God. This Kingdom of God we speak of, we have to learn to look upon as an absolute monarchy, wherein one will is supreme, and beyond which is the outer darkness, where all is confusion and dismay. And the peculiar discipline we have each of us to go through in this life is to learn submission to the supreme will. . . . It seems a strange thing that a lifetime should be spent in this, and that the very highest employment of the will of man is to surrender willingly to God's will, but so it is."

In a further reading on "Sufficiency of Grace in God," Marcus Dods writes:

"Learning as we do to take our own measure, we become convinced of our littleness, of our incapacity to shine, our inability to remove ignorance, our helplessness in presence of surrounding and oppressive darkness.

"When we become profoundly convinced of our blundering methods, of our beating the air, of the feeble and inefficient assaults we make upon the dense masses of evil around us, when we are saddened by our own incompetence and futility, there are reasonable grounds which should recall us to more hopeful thoughts. For all the work required of us there is an unfailing supply of grace.

"We are not called upon to create a holy spirit for ourselves. Holiness sufficient for all moral beings exists in God. There is that in Him which can sustain in goodness the spirit of each. The Holy Spirit is equal to all demands that can be made upon Him. The Holy Spirit is God so that as there is in God life enough for all creatures, a strength sufficient to maintain in being all that is, so there is in God a holiness sufficient for the need of all. There is strength and grace enough in God to carry through the whole work that this world requires. In God there is patience, love, wisdom, sacrifice—in a word, goodness enough for the overcoming of all evil."

Take the Lowest Seat

Woe unto you, Pharisees! for ye love the uppermost seats in the syna-gogues, and greetings in the markets (Luke 11:43).

NOTHING causes more trouble in churches than the desire for the highest seat. The mother of James and John thought that her request for them to sit on the right and left hand of the Lord in His glory was most laudable, but the Lord Jesus replied that that position was in the Father's hand and was for those who could drink the cup of suffering, shame, humiliation, and obloquy. —Lillian Harvey.

There is wreck and ruin in the path of every place-hunter unless the place he is hunting is at the foot of the Cross coupled with willingness to be used any place God may direct. No professed follower of Christ can seek his own glory without robbing Christ of the glory that rightfully belongs to Him. A large share of trouble and divisions in churches, and a frightful number of souls lost to God and the church, may be attributed to work and influence of the place-hunter. —Unknown.

> While place we seek or place we shun
> The soul finds happiness in none,
> But with a God to guide our way,
> 'Tis equal joy to go or stay.
> —Madam Guyon.

The *Christian Digest* tells this most interesting story: "When the Queen of England was nine years old she went shopping with her regal grandmother, Queen Mary, in some of London's most impressive stores. Crowds gathered outside the stores waiting for a glimpse of the beloved little Princess when she should reappear.

"Small Elizabeth became very impatient at the time her grandmother was spending with her purchases. She urged,

'Please hurry, Grandmother. I wish to go out and let all those people see me.'

"Sorrowfully, Queen Mary led little Elizabeth to a rear exit of the store. They returned to Buckingham Palace by a devious route.

"'England must never see one of its princesses when she is full of foolish conceit, my child,' Elizabeth was told. 'England loves your father and mother because they serve, not because they rule. Never forget that, Elizabeth. Your loveliest crown is not made of gold and precious stones, but of humility.'"

Plato has said that "only those who do not desire power are fit to hold it." The best rulers are those who rule unwillingly. "Let those follow the pursuits of ambition and fame," said Washington, "who have a keener relish for them, or who may have more years in store for the enjoyment." Thus he wrote at fifty-seven years of age. Washington wished for a quiet life, but by the unanimous vote of the people he was recalled to the high position of the President. It was with a heavy heart, however, that he accepted the nation's call to take the highest seat.

Luther said, "Never are men more unfit than when they think themselves most fit, and best prepared for their duty; never more fit, than when most humbled and ashamed under a sense of their own unfitness."

> What is all righteousness that men devise?
> What, but a sordid bargain for the skies?
> But Christ as soon would abdicate His own,
> As stoop from Heaven to sell the proud a throne.
> —William Cowper.

The person with true humility never has to be shown his place; he is always in it. —Opal Fitzgerald.

Keep Out of Sight

I am crucified with Christ: nevertheless I live; yet not I, but Christ liveth in me: and the life which I now live in the flesh I live by the faith of the Son of God, who loved me, and gave himself for me (Gal. 2:20).

HAROLD St. John, a very excellent Bible teacher in England, illustrates the above thought in a short extract: "A minister of the Gospel went to visit a lighthouse keeper, who dwelt on a rock some fifteen miles off the coast. On arrival, he was told he would find the keeper up in the tower. He climbed up and found his friend busy polishing the reflectors; in his ignorance he supposed that this was in honor of his visit and said: 'Mr.____ do not bother polishing those things, I did not come to see them but you.'

"With a twinkle in his eye he replied: 'Young man, we do not polish reflectors that they may be seen, but that they may not be seen. A reflector that can be seen is a bad reflector.'

"A lesson we all need to learn is that it is in the obliteration of self that we make others see the glory of the Light of the world. Reflectors catch the rays from the great light and flash them over the dark waters."

An old fisherman was sitting by a stream abounding in trout. His equipment was most primitive, but he was catching one fish after another. An onlooker who had walked up and down the stream noticed that others with more sophisticated fishing rods were unsuccessful.

Curious, the visitor asked the old man what was his formula for success. Placing his crooked stick into the ground, he sat back and surveyed the young man who was looking a bit disdainfully at the old primitive fishing rod and said: "There are three secrets. The first: keep yourself out of sight. The second: keep yourself further out of sight, and the third: keep yourself still further out of sight."

I wonder what impresses folks;
    I wonder what they see
In what I do or feel or say;
    Is it, Lord, You or me?

What is it that they really feel
    About me when I've gone —
That I am great or kind or good,
    Or that I know Your Son?

Dear Lord, I feel it really is
    A useless life to live,
If what I AM is all that I
    Have got inside to give.

Then may I, crucified in Love
    To all I say or do,
Make others think not of myself,
    But only, Lord, of You.
                     — Trudy Tait.

That humility which courts notice is not first-rate. It may be sincere, but it is sullied. Do not sound a trumpet or say: "Come and see how humble I am." — Cecil.

It takes the Almighty God to make us so absolutely His that we do not desire to be noticed. — Anon.

It is an untold mercy to escape parade in print. I believe that offends God very often and mars the permanence of the work. To work on quietly, and trust God for fruit that shall remain, I feel more and more sure that this is the right way. — Thomas Walker of Tinnevelly.

Admit Your Size

I am the least of the apostles (1 Cor. 15:9).
Unto me, who am less than the least of all saints, is this grace given
(Eph. 3:8).

THE Apostle Paul, at one time in his life, had an experience in which he passed into the third heavens. And yet,
though he could boast of more learning and prestige than
could the other apostles, his testimony after receiving this marvelous vision was that he was "less than the least." One could
not get much smaller!

This reminds us of the story of a little girl who walked
down a city street hand in hand with her father. "Daddy, what
are those boys doing up there," asked the little one as she
viewed men working on a scaffold some twenty storeys high.
The father replied that they were not boys, but men who
looked like boys because they were up so high. Thinking
deeply, his daughter looked up very seriously into her father's
face saying, "They won't amount to much when they get to
Heaven, will they?" — Lillian Harvey.

I am learning here how to estimate myself with more
modesty. I had lived in a sphere where I was everything, had
never gone out of my sphere to see how the broad world lived.
Here I am in London, and who am I here? It is good for me —
I feel it to be good; in one view just the thing I wanted. It does
not crush me or anything like that, but it shows me what a
speck I am. Anything that makes us know the world better and
our relations to it, the ways of reaching mankind, what popularity is worth, how large the world is, and how many little
things it takes to fill it with an influence — anything which sets
a man practically in his place is a mental good.

— Horace Bushnell.

Will Crooks had just been elected leader of the British Labor Party. He decided that he would take his little daughter to Westminster to show her its beauty. Seemingly awed by the splendor of the Abbey, the little girl remained silent for a time. The father, desirous to know what impression had been made upon the little one asked, "What are you thinking so deeply about, dear?" He got an answer he least expected: "I was thinking, daddy, that you're a big man in our kitchen, but you aren't very much here."

Opinion of ourselves is like the casting of a shadow, which is always longest when the sun is at the greatest distance. By the degrees that the sun approaches, the shadow shortens, and under the direct meridian light, it becomes none at all. It is so with our opinion of ourselves. While the good influences of God are at the greatest distance from us, it is then always that we conceive best of ourselves. As God approaches, the conceit lessens, till we receive the fuller measures of His grace, and then we become nothing, in our own conceit, and God appears to be all in all. —Dean Young.

> Less, less of self each day
>   And more, my God, of Thee;
> Oh, keep me in Thy way,
>   However rough it be.
>
> More moulded to Thy will,
>   Lord, let Thy servant be;
> Higher and higher still—
>   Nearer and nearer Thee.
>   —Unknown.

"Every man has a right to be conceited until he is successful," said Disraeli. In God's service, however, God will not entrust spiritual success to any servant of His until they have taken His judicial sentence upon themselves that "Apart from me ye can do nothing."

Take Heed of Climbing

LORD, my heart is not haughty, nor mine eyes lofty: neither do I exercise myself in great matters, or in things too high for me (Psalms 131:1).

PINNACLES of the temple are places of temptation. . . . High places are slippery places; advancement in the world makes a man a fair mark for Satan to shoot his fiery darts at. God casts down that He may raise up; the devil raiseth up that he may cast down: therefore, those that would take heed of falling, must take heed of climbing. High places in the Church are in a special manner dangerous. Those that excel in gifts, are in eminent stations, and have gained a great reputation, have need to keep humble, for Satan will be sure to aim at them, to puff them up with pride, and so they "fall into the condemnation of the devil"; those that stand high are concerned to stand fast. —Unknown.

There is no better time for the exercise of humility than when we succeed. —Mary Lyon.

A. Tholuck was a professor in Halle University, Germany, who greatly influenced his students to live upright, godly lives. This learned man utters the identical truths which many other saints have learned for he was a student at the same school of humility. He bares his heart to us in the following:

"The desire for great things is deeply implanted in all our hearts. To whom has it not occasioned a fall! Upward, upward, each one presses, forgetting that the Word of Truth says, 'He that humbleth himself shall be exalted.' How much less is our spiritual danger if we remain in a lowly condition. The heart is not so closely tied to the things of earth, and we can more readily and willingly depart. We are less fettered by the pleasures of sense; we are more sober and watchful unto prayer.

"Many a one, when he thought himself secure, has been ensnared by high things and insensibly fallen into a serving of the flesh, which has destroyed his inner life. Again, in lowly circumstances, how much more readily we acknowledge ourselves to be nothing. I felt how very difficult it is for men to exercise authority without sinning. So long as our heart is not wholly devoted to God, Satan persuades us that the honor and the homage which we receive from those who are under us, belong to us, and not to the Lord.

"Lord, I confess how guilty I am, in that I often repine because Thou dost not allow me to rise another step higher; how guilty I am, in that I do not love the lowly condition, since Thou Thyself didst choose and hallow it. How can I fear to be numbered among the unknown and mean of the earth, when I remember that Thou, the King of glory, from love to us hast not disdained them, and that whoever, in true contentedness of heart, has communion also with Thee? Among the great ones of the earth, Thou hast so seldom had Thy true disciples, but hast found them among those who have been the weak and base and despised of the world."

When reason contradicts Thy law, or climbs
    So high, she weeneth to know more than Thou,
Break down her confidence, great God, betimes,
    And teach her lowly at Thy feet to bow.
Nor let my proud heart dictate, Lord, to Thee,
    But tame the wayward will that seeks its own,
    And wake the love that clings to Thee alone
And takes Thy judgments in humility.
—Unknown.

Pride never stoops but to take a higher flight.
—Unknown.

We sink into nothingness as we grow up into Christ.
—R. C. Chapman.

The Strappado

Hezekiah rendered not again according to the benefit done unto him; for his heart was lifted up: therefore there was wrath upon him, and upon Judah and Jerusalem (2 Chron. 32:25).
All my bones are out of joint (Psa. 22:14).

IN old and evil days, there was a diabolical instrument of torture in Spain, called the Strappado. And that cruel instrument was worked in this wicked way. The poor victim was first hoisted up to a great height, by means of ropes and pulleys, and then he was suddenly dashed to the ground, till every bone in his body was torn out of joint and broken in pieces. And the name of the Spanish strappado has passed into the English language, because the old preachers of that day frequently employed the illustration of the strappado in their experimental sermons, as does Goodwin: "Now, his lusts, both of body and mind, do strappado a sinner's expectations. That is to say: his sinful imaginations hoist up his expectations of pleasure to a great height, and then, suddenly, he is let fall. For when the sinner comes to enjoy his high expectations, they always prove themselves to be such flat empty things, that his soul, being completely cheated, says to itself—'And is this all!' Thus, always, do a sinner's high expectations strappado him, till his spirit is simply dashed to pieces within him."

So far as I know, the Spanish strappado was never imported into Scotland or England. But if we have not the scaffoldings, and the pulleys, and the ropes, of that inhuman instrument among us, we have plenty of those personal experiences which are so vividly and so forcibly illustrated by those scaffoldings and pulleys, and ropes and broken bones. For we have plenty of high expectations followed by deep disappointments; plenty of great and towering ambitions, followed by great depressions; plenty of high hopes followed by low despairs; plenty of seekings of great things for ourselves, followed by small and heart-starving results. Till it has been powerfully impressed upon me that the Spanish strappado may have some important lessons to read to us in our own land, and in our own day. . . .

What a strappado the pursuit of praise and fame is to many men among us. . . . A friend of mine, a minister in England, became absolutely intoxicated with the ambition to write a great book on a great subject. When, after years of neglect of his pulpit and his pastorate in his devotion to his book, he was in Edinburgh and called on me, for hour after hour he poured out to me about his coming masterpiece. But when it came out, his book only received one little scurvy review in one obscure London newspaper. When I next saw my friend, I scarcely knew him, so shrunk was he both in body and in mind. He was like our text: he had had such a fall that all his bones were out of joint.

You will often see the same thing in preachers and public speakers. A member of Assembly, say, has labored for weeks at a great speech, which is to make his reputation. But when he enters the advertised hall, the house is empty. And he suffers such a fall from his pride that moment that he can scarcely command his strength enough to finish the fourth part of what he had written with such labor and expectation.

The pulpit also is the sure strappado of the popular-hunting preacher. Even if he is puffed up for a time, the time soon comes for another to arise who wholly eclipses him, till he lies with broken bones at the foot of his forgotten and forsaken pulpit. The higher his ambition hoisted him up, the deeper and more heartbreaking is his fall. Let these examples of strappado suffice. Every man whose eyes are open will see plenty of such examples all around him. And he is a happy man who is not such an example himself. — Alexander Whyte in *With Mercy and With Judgment.*

> Lord, give me grace
> To take the lowest place;
> Nor even desire,
> Unless it be Thy will, to go up higher.
> — Unknown.

Too Big To Be Little

A man's pride shall bring him low: but honour shall uphold the humble in spirit (Prov. 29:23).

ONE of the last messages of G. Fred Bergin, director of the Müller Orphan Homes in Bristol, was: "Tell my younger brethren that they may be too big for God to use them, but they cannot be too small."

"Too big for God to use me!" O Lord, forgive my sin,
And let the pride that hinders be taken from within.
So much of self in service the blessing cannot come,
And thus the work is useless which I had thought well done.

"Too big for God to use me!" This is the reason why
Poor longing souls are famished who come, and go, and die!
O God my Savior, help me in deep humility
To make a full surrender henceforth to own but Thee.

"Too big for God to use me!" But if I am possessed
With unction through His Spirit, then shall my work be blessed;
I'll count myself as nothing, seek Christ to magnify,
And use my gifts in service, my Lord to glorify.
    —*Message from God.*

William Bramwell was a man of prayer, often spending weeks communing with Heaven before going into a campaign. He was honored by God with powerful results. The reason — he was solely dependent upon God for all his efforts — not upon eloquence, or learning, or influence among the honorable, but upon the Spirit of God working upon human hearts. A few extracts from his letters will reveal the conception this man had of his own abilities.

"I grow. I am less. I become more ashamed, and more dependent upon my heavenly Father. My fellowship with

God is closer, more constant, and with stronger affection. I am the most grieved with my preaching. It is so far short of the subject—Redemption, Full Salvation. I tremble as much as ever, and the modesty put upon my soul makes me tremble in the presence of the people. I am using every means by prayer, etc., to be fit to live among angels. O how pure, how holy, must they be in Heaven!"

"I mean that the soul never be diverted from Him for one moment, but that I view Him in all my acts, take hold of Him as the Instrument by which I do all my work, and feel that nothing is done without Him. To seek man, world, self-praise is so shocking to my view at present that I wonder we are not all struck dead when the least of this comes upon us!"

"Never imagine that you have arrived at the summit. No, see God in all things, and you will see NO END."

"O for this mighty faith that brings the blessing! When you receive this you will be less than ever. You will feel your nothingness but your all from God and in God."

Molinos, the Spanish saint, quaintly portrays true humility: "The true humility doth not consist in external acts, in taking the lowest place, in going in poor clothes, in speaking submissively, in shutting the eyes, in affectionate sighings, nor in condemning thy ways, calling thyself miserable to give others to understand that thou art humble.

"It consists only in the contempt of thyself and the desire to be despised, with a low and profound knowledge, without concerning thyself whether thou art esteemed or no. The torment of light, wherewith the Lord with His graces enlightens the soul, doth two things: it discovers the greatness of God, and at the same time the soul knows its own misery, insomuch that no tongue is able to express the depth in which it is overwhelmed, being desirous that everyone should know its humility; and it is so far from vain-glory and complacency, as it sees that grace of God to be mere goodness of Him, and nothing but His mercy which is pleased to take pity on it."

Emptiness Before Filling

The Almighty hath dealt very bitterly with me. I went out full, and the LORD hath brought me home again empty (Ruth 1:20,21).

WE hear much about the filling of the Spirit, but we do not hear too much about the emptying process which must precede it. Naomi's lament has been that of every Christian who has gone on with the Lord. We all go out full; full of ourselves, our calling, our gifts, our successes and are "brought home empty."

Naomi was indeed emptied — bereft of husband and two sons, possessing no grandchildren — with just two daughters-in-law who now, widowed, were free to seek a husband among their own people. Bitterly, Naomi considered her plight. Little did she know that although she was returning empty, she was introducing into Bethlehem a young Moabitish maiden who would become an important figure in the line of the long-looked-for Messiah.

Ruth's utter dedication is unmatched in its beauty of total and complete resignation to God when no earthly consideration at that time could have been a motivation for reward.

The story of Ruth and Naomi is not the only incident in Scripture where emptiness had to precede filling. *Empty* pitchers were used by Gideon to defeat the Midianites. The widow was told by Elisha to provide *empty* vessels "not a few," and their miraculous filling brought her out of bankruptcy. The rich, Christ sent *empty* away for they had no vacuum which Christ could fill with Himself. He Who was our example, "*emptied* Himself of all but love, and died for Adam's helpless race." — Lillian Harvey.

Paul Gerhardt expressed his sentiments in this beautiful hymn, translated from the German:

"Thus though worn, and tried, and tempted,
    Glorious calling, saint, is thine;
Let the Lord but find thee emptied,
    Living branch in Christ, the Vine!
Vessels of the world's despising,
    Vessels weak, and poor, and base,
Bearing wealth God's heart is prizing,
    Glory from Christ's blessed face.

"Oh to be but emptier, lowlier,
    Mean, unnoticed, and unknown,
And to God a vessel holier,
    Filled with Christ and Christ alone!
Naught of earth to cloud the glory,
    Naught of self the light to dim,
Telling forth His wondrous story,
    Emptied, to be filled with Him."

Some living creatures maintain their hold by foot or body on flat surfaces by a method that seems like magic and with a tenacity that amazes the observer. A fly marching at ease with feet uppermost on a plastered ceiling, a mollusc sticking to the smooth water-worn surface of a basaltic rock, while the long swell of the Atlantic at every pulse sends a huge white billow roaring and hissing and cracking and crunching over it, are objects of wonder to the onlooker. That apparently supernatural solidity is the most natural thing in the world. It is emptiness that imparts so much strength to these feeble creatures. A vacuum on the one side within a web-foot, and on the other within the shell, is the secret of their power. By dint of that emptiness in itself, the creature quietly and easily clings to the wall or the rock, so making all the strength of the wall or rock its own. By the emptiness it is held fast; the moment it becomes full, it drops off. Ah! It is the self-emptiness of a humble, trustful soul that makes the Redeemer's strength his own, and so keeps him safe in an evil world. — W. Arnot.

He that is little in his own eyes will not be troubled to be little in the eye of others. — Ralph Venning, 1620-73.

Triumphant Defeat

But ye shall not be so: but he that is greatest among you, let him be as the younger; and he that is chief, as he that doth serve (Luke 22:26).

IT is not often that modesty is persuasive. A submissive demeanor is not an eloquent thing to the generality of men. If God does not make a noise in His own world, He is ignored. If He does, He is considered unseasonable and oppressive. . . .

His was a life of weakness. Helplessness, humiliation, and a kind of shame were round about Him. He chose them as His first created state. This choice was one of the primary laws of the Incarnation, as a mission to fallen man. He clung to it through the Three-and-Thirty Years. He made it to be the supernatural condition of His Church, that sort of continual triumphant defeat in which her life so visibly consists. He perpetuated it for Himself in the Blessed Sacrament. It was as if weakness was so new to Omnipotence, that there was an attraction in its novelty. To show forth power in weakness, to be feeble and yet to be strong also, and not only strong together with the weakness, but actually because of it—this was to display one of those hidden and nameless perfections in God, which we should perhaps never have seen except by the light of the Incarnation. . . .

Our Lord's Divinity appears to hinder anything from becoming a humiliation. It raises ignominies into worshipful mysteries. It clothes shame with a beauty which beams so brightly that it almost hides from us the horror of the outrage. His lowness becomes a divine height, a height which none could reach but God. His disgraces are crowned with luster and become nobilities. He raises what He touches to His own height; it does not sink Him to its vileness.

The Jews failed to recognize the dignity and royalty which lay beneath that outward garb of humiliation. Their discernment was gone. They were blinded by the very spiritual magnificence of their ancient prophecies. They were looking in all directions rather than toward the Cave of Bethlehem, and when Messias came, He was their scandal rather than their hope; and, while they shed their own blood for pretenders, they spilt the blood of their true King in disappointment and disgust. The gorgeous martial procession which was to go forth to conquer and redeem the world, will issue from the cave of Bethlehem, but the fallen people have no eye to recognize the celestial splendor of that new manner of warfare, whose triumphs are in the depths of its abasement. . . .

The strong man is he who has gone deepest down into the weakness of Christ. The enduring work is that which Christ's humiliation has touched secretly and made it almost omnipotent. . . . The soul is hampered by material helps. Strength is in fewness. Work lies in singleness of purpose. The victory is with him who has nothing to lose, and if so be, needs less than the nothing he has got. Though God Himself is untold wealth, riches are not godlike. For it is not so much that God has wealth, as that He is His own wealth. They are rich who possess God, but they are richest who possess nothing but God. All creation belongs to him to whom God is his sole possession. — F. W. Faber, from *Bethlehem*.

> Blessed Savior, Christ most holy,
>   In a manger Thou didst rest;
> Canst Thou stoop again, yet lower,
>   And abide within my breast?. . .
>
> Enter, then, O Christ most holy;
>   Make a Christmas in my heart;
> Make a Heaven of my manger:
>   It is Heaven where Thou art.
>   — George Stringer Rowe.

Humbling Before Honor

The fear of the LORD is the instruction of wisdom; and before honour is humility (Prov. 15:33).

Before destruction the heart of a man is haughty, and before honour is humility (Prov. 18:12).

THE wind goeth toward the south, and turneth about unto the north; it whirleth about continually, and the wind returneth again according to his circuits" (Eccl. 1:6). Commenting on this verse, George Warnock said: "The same old wind going through its various circuits! Yes, but not really so. It blows in one direction as the north wind. Then it completes the cycle, becomes the south wind, and blows back from whence it started. God's order is first darkness, then light. First chaos, then order. First barrenness, then fruitfulness. First weakness, then power. First death, then life.

"Never have we heard so much about positive living as we have in the past decade or two, and never has there been so much frustration amongst God's people. We have come to believe, somehow, that anything that speaks of coldness or barrenness or fruitlessness is from the devil and must be strenuously resisted. We are encouraged to reach forth and grasp the glory, and the power, and the victory, and the fruit of the Spirit.

"The fact is we are negative by nature, and victory is not ours by blindly refusing to acknowledge our own futility, and vainly attempting to arouse some secret potential of our character within. This might have its place in the realm of this world system, but not in the realm of God. God is consistently seeking to bring us to the place where we recognize the utter nothingness and futility of our whole being and way of life by nature. For it is in the full recognition of all that we are in the realm of weakness and failure that we may reach out and grasp hold of the Divine promises.

"It is only when Jacob is smitten in the place of strength, 'in the hollow of his thigh,' that he finally submits to defeat, and clings to the angel of God. And it is only in his defeat and in clinging to the angel after his defeat, that his name is changed from one of weakness to one of power with God.

"We are thankful to see that there is a certain restlessness and dissatisfaction in the hearts of those who are pressing on with the Lord. We are speaking of those who are walking with God and therefore sharing His secrets. These are the ones who are being 'marked' in this day and hour, by the man with the inkhorn at his side. 'And the Lord said unto him, Go through the midst of the city, through the midst of Jerusalem, and set a mark upon the foreheads of the men that sigh and that cry for all the abominations that be done in the midst thereof'" (Ezek. 9:4). — George H. Warnock in *Refiner's Fire*. Used by permission.

Martin Luther came to the same conclusion to which all God's true men have come when he said: "It is the nature of God to make something out of nothing; therefore, when anyone is nothing, God may yet make something of him.

"Whom God chooses to make wise, He first makes a fool; Whom He chooses to make strong, He first renders weak. He delivers to death the man whom He means to quicken; He depresses to Hell whomsoever He intends to call to Heaven."

We *are* nothing unless we abide in God; we can *do* nothing apart from Christ. We know and admit this as a doctrine, but to realize it as a fact, painful and humbling experience is often needed. But in this lowest humiliation is our true and highest exaltation. God takes all things from us that we may turn again to Him as our sure Portion; He makes us feel our weakness, our poverty, our ignorance, in order that we may return to Him.
— Adolph Saphir in *The Hidden Life*.

All desire to be humble, but few desire to be humbled.
— Anon.

Rejection Before Acceptance

He is despised and rejected of men; a man of sorrows, and acquainted with grief: and we hid as it were our faces from him; he was despised, and we esteemed him not (Isa. 53:3).

ONE of my intimate ministerial friends had an experience which has suggested the title of this chapter. His congregation persistently refused to accept his message. He wanted to lead his flock into the green pastures and beside the still waters, but they were unwilling to be led. His choir, with their ungodly practices, brought things to a crisis.

The position had become so unbearable that he invited the choir to resign, for he felt like one of old, whenever he attempted to preach, that "Satan stood at his right hand to resist him." The choir not only resigned but persuaded the congregation to desist from taking any part in the singing.

The result was that whatever singing was done had to be done by the preacher, the choir and congregation rejoicing in his discomfiture and refusing to join. This state of things continued for some time, and, quite naturally, my friend was greatly dejected and perplexed at the turn events had taken. He was at his wits' end when God spoke to him. He was sitting one day on a seat in a park when he saw before him on the ground part of a torn newspaper. That torn paper had a message for him that exactly suited his need. It was this: *"No man is ever fully accepted until he has, first of all, been utterly rejected."*

He needed nothing more. He had been utterly rejected, and his recognition of the fact was the beginning of a most fruitful ministry in another sphere which continues unto this day, and proves how fully he had been accepted by God though so utterly rejected by man.

It was so with Dr. A. B. Simpson of New York, the founder of the Christian and Missionary Alliance. This is how Dr.

Simpson himself describes the second of these crises: "I look back with unutterable gratitude to the lonely and sorrowful night when, mistaken in many things and imperfect in all, and not knowing but that it would be death in the most literal sense before the morning light, my heart's first full consecration was made, and with unreserved surrender I first could say:

> 'Jesus, I my cross have taken,
>   All to leave and follow Thee;
> Destitute, despised, forsaken,
>   Thou, from hence, my all shalt be.'

"Never, perhaps, has my heart known such a thrill of joy as when the following Sabbath morning I gave out those lines and sung them with all my heart."

Dr. Simpson had to learn later, when in response to the call of God he resigned his pastorate, what it really meant to be "destitute, despised, forsaken." "He surrendered a (then) lucrative salary of $5,000.00; a position as a leading pastor in the greatest American city, and all claim upon his denomination for assistance in a yet untried work. He was in a great city with no following, no organization, no financial resources, with a large family dependent upon him, and with his most intimate ministerial friends and former associates predicting failure." So completely was he misunderstood, even by those from whom he expected sympathy, that he once said he often looked down upon the paving stones in the streets for the sympathy that was denied him elsewhere.

The rugged path of utter rejection was trodden not only uncomplainingly but with rejoicing. —Gregory Mantle in *Beyond Humiliation.*

> Beware of too sublime a sense
> Of your own worth and consequence.
> The man who dreams himself so great,
> And his importance of such weight,
> That all around in all that's done
> Must move and act for him alone,
> Will learn in school of tribulation
> The folly of his expectation.
>   — William Cowper.

Reduced to Despair

We were pressed out of measure, above strength, insomuch that we despaired even of life (2 Cor. 1:8).

YOU can't in preaching produce at the same time," said James Denney, "the impression that you are clever and that Christ is wonderful." Perhaps few men would have had more right to impress their audience with their genius than Professor Denney, principal of Glasgow College and considered one of the most distinguished scholars and preachers of his day. In a Brethren periodical, Touchstone gives us a further glimpse of this remarkable man:

"James Moffatt said of him that he impressed people with the consciousness of 'being far more than anything he said, or did, or wrote, no matter how you admired those products of his mind.'. . . He was said to know thoroughly seven different languages. He could quote the New Testament with as much ease in the original as in English. . . .

"He wrote much in the *Expositor* and the *British Weekly*, though his books are his most enduring memorial. Dr. Campbell Morgan used to describe his book *The Death of Christ* as, perhaps, the greatest written exposition of the Atonement."

The following extract from one of his commentaries shows why God often deems it necessary to reduce us to despair.

"The Apostle, who has a divine gift for interpreting experience and reading its lessons, tells us why he and his friends had to pass such a terrible time. It was that they might trust, not in themselves, but in God Who raises the dead. It is natural, he implies, for us to trust in ourselves. It is so natural, and so confirmed by the habits of a lifetime, that no ordinary difficulty or perplexities avail to break us of it. It takes all God can do to root up our self-confidence. He must reduce us to despair. . . . It is out of this despair that the superhuman hope is born. It is out of this abject helplessness that the soul learns to look up with new trust to God. . . .

115

"How do most of us attain to any faith in Providence? Is it not by proving through numberless experiments, that it is not in man that walketh to direct his steps? Is it not by coming, again and again, to the limit of our resources, and being compelled to feel that unless there is a wisdom and a love at work on our behalf, immeasurably wiser and more benignant than our own, life is a moral chaos? How, above all, do we come to any faith in Redemption? To any abiding trust in Jesus Christ as the Savior of our souls? Is it not by this same way of despair? Is it not by the profound consciousness that in ourselves there is no answer to the question, How shall man be just with God? and that the answer must be sought in Him?

"Is it not by failure, by defeat, by deep disappointments, by ominous forebodings hardening into the awful certainty that we cannot with our own resources make ourselves good men — is it not by experiences like these that we are led to the Cross? . . .

"Only desperation opens our eyes to God's love. We do not heartily own Him as the Author of Life and Health, unless He has raised us from our sickness after the doctor has given us up. We do not acknowledge His paternal guidance of our life, unless in some sudden peril, or some impending disaster, He provides an unexpected deliverance. We do not confess that salvation is of the Lord, until our very soul has been convinced that in it there dwells no good thing. Happy are those who are taught even by despair, to set their hope in God; and who, when they learn this lesson once, learn it like St. Paul, once for all.

"Faith and hope like those which burn through this Epistle were well worth purchasing, even at such a price; they were blessings so valuable that the love of God did not shrink from reducing Paul to despair that he might be compelled to grasp them. Let us believe when such trials come into our lives — when we are weighed down exceedingly beyond our strength, and are in darkness without light, in a valley of the shadow of death with no outlet — that God is not dealing with us cruelly or at random, but shutting us up to an experience of His love which we have hitherto declined."

Genius Balanced with Thorns

Lest I should be exalted above measure through the abundance of the revelations, there was given to me a thorn in the flesh, the messenger of Satan to buffet me, lest I should be exalted above measure (2 Cor. 12:7).

ROBERT Hall, born in 1764 and contemporary with the Baptist missionary, William Carey, possessed a genius in the pulpit that was unparalleled. He could so move his audience that they would, at times, rise from their seats and stand until the preacher had uttered his last words. It is perhaps not surprising that such a talented young orator was given thorns in the flesh to balance those outstanding gifts which might otherwise have tended to self exaltation.

"When a young man has displayed exceptional talents from his earliest days," says his biographer, "his achievements inevitably call forth the admiration of all who know him. This was the case with Robert and it was, therefore, not surprising that such admiration and praise had gone to his head a little, producing a certain amount of self-assurance and conceit. Although it was not an unduly prominent flaw in his character, sooner or later the bubble of his vanity was sure to be pricked. It speaks well for his fundamental good sense, however, that when humiliation did come his way, he was able to take the lesson to heart.

"It was the custom for the Academy students to preach in rotation before the tutors and their fellow-students, and when Robert's turn arrived, he stood up on the platform in a Broadmead vestry to deliver a sermon, without notes, as required. . . . The young preacher began well and his congregation prepared to sit back in obvious appreciation. Suddenly, he hesitated. There was a long pause. In startled attention, the others looked up, realizing something was wrong. Then, amid an uncomfortable and embarrassed silence, they saw Robert fling up his hands to cover his face. 'Oh! I have lost all my ideas!' he cried. . . . The gathering was hastily dismissed and

Robert was told not to take his failure too much to heart, but to make another attempt the next week.

"The following week he stood before his congregation again, and to their astonishment the same distressing scene was repeated. Shamed and humiliated, his face scarlet, Robert rushed out of the room and was heard to exclaim as he went through the doorway, 'If this does not humble me, the devil must have me!'"

"Such," declared a friend, "were the early efforts of him whose humility afterwards became as conspicuous as his talents, and who, for nearly half a century, excited universal admiration by the splendor of his pulpit eloquence."

"The remarkable modesty and affability of his deportment presented an affecting contrast to the splendor of his genius," adds another contemporary. And his biographer continues: "The vanity of his youth he had learned to overcome, and forever after he abhorred it in everyone else, to such an extent that his comments upon conceit could be blistering."

It is not surprising that God allowed this able genius to experience certain physical disabilities which kept him totally dependent upon the Holy Spirit. Such disabilities, at times, almost incapacitated him for his high calling. While in the pulpit, his pain was so aggravated that he would clutch his back with one of his hands. This same affliction so disturbed his night hours, that often he would rise from bed to sleep between two chairs.

Pain, however, has a wonderful knack of showing us how very weak we are, and so it was with Robert Hall. His years of suffering reveal their fruit in a letter to a friend, written when forty-two years of age. He attributes all his gifts to One — even the Almighty: "If my ministry has been at all blessed as the means of spiritual good to your soul, God alone is entitled to the praise. I have been, in every sense of the word, an unprofitable servant. When I consider the value of souls, the preciousness of the blood of Christ, and the weight of eternal things, I am ashamed and astonished to think I could have spoken on such subjects with so little impression, and that I did not travail in birth more, till Christ was formed in my hearers."

God Resisteth the Proud

God resisteth the proud, but giveth grace unto the humble (James 4:6).

RICHARD Baxter, the Puritan preacher and writer, labored under a burden of ill-health all his life. He attributed much of his usefulness to the fact that he ministered as a dying man to dying men with a constant sense of eternity ever before him. The following is an excerpt from the book, *The Saints' Everlasting Rest,* which he wrote on what he thought was his dying bed:

"There is such an antipathy between this (a proud spirit) and God, that thou wilt never get thy heart near Him, nor get Him near thy heart, as long as this prevaileth in it. If it cast the angels out of Heaven, it must needs keep thy heart from Heaven. If it cast our first parents out of paradise, separated between the Lord and us and brought His curse on all the creatures here below, it will certainly keep our hearts from Paradise and increase the cursed separation from our God.

"Intercourse with God will keep men low, and that low-liness will promote their intercourse. When a man is used to being much with God and taken up with the study of His glorious attributes, he abhors himself in dust and ashes. And that self-abhorrence is his best preparative to obtain admittance to God again.

"Therefore after a soul-humbling day or in times of trouble, when the soul is lowest, it useth to have freest access to God and savor most of the life above. The delight of God is in 'him that is poor and of a contrite spirit, and trembleth at (His) word,' and the delight of such a soul is in God. Where there is mutual delight there will be freest admittance, heartiest welcome, and frequent converse.

"But God is so far from dwelling in the soul that is proud that He will not admit it to any near access. A proud mind is high in conceit, self-esteem, and carnal aspiring; a humble

119

mind is high indeed in God's esteem and in holy aspiring. These two sorts of high-mindedness are most of all opposite to each other, as we see most wars are between princes and princes and not between a prince and a plowman.

"Well then, art thou a man of worth in thine own eyes? Art thou delighted when thou hearest of thy esteem with men and much dejected when thou hearest that they slight thee? Dost thou love those best that honor thee and think meanly of them that do not, though they be otherwise men of godliness and honesty? Must thou have thy humors fulfilled and thy judgment be a rule, and thy word a law to all about thee? Are thy passions kindled if thy word or will be crossed?

"Art thou ready to judge humility to be sordid business, and knowest not how to submit to humble confession when thou hast sinned against God or injured thy brother? Art thou one that lookest strangely at the godly poor and art almost ashamed to be their companion? Canst thou not serve God in a low place as well as a high? Are thy boastings restrained more by prudence or artifice than by humility? Dost thou desire to have all men's eyes upon thee and to hear them say, 'This is he?. . .'

"O Christian! if thou wouldst live continually in the presence of thy Lord, lie in the dust and He will thence take thee up. Learn of Him to be meek and lowly, and thou shalt find rest unto thy soul. Otherwise thou shalt be 'like the troubled sea, when it cannot rest, whose waters cast up mire and dirt.' Instead of these sweet delights in God, thy pride will fill thee with perpetual disquiet.

"As he that humbleth himself as a little child shall be greatest in the Kingdom of Heaven, so shall he now be greatest in the foretastes of that Kingdom."

"The dust and Heaven are the only safe places for the believer," said an old preacher, "and of the two, the dust is the safer; for the angels fell from Heaven, but no one was ever known to fall from the dust."

Pride Is Competitive

They measuring themselves by themselves, and comparing themselves among themselves, are not wise (2 Cor. 10:12).

ACCORDING to Christian teachers, the essential vice, the utmost evil, is Pride. Unchastity, anger, greed, drunkenness, and all that, are mere fleabites in comparison; it was through Pride that the devil became the devil. Pride leads to every other vice; it is the complete anti-God state of mind. . . .

Does this seem to you exaggerated? . . . If you want to find out how proud you are, the easiest way is to ask yourself, "How much do I dislike it when other people snub me, or refuse to take any notice of me, or shove their oar in, or patronize me, or show off?" The point is that each person's pride is in competition with everyone else's pride. It is because I wanted to be the big noise at the party that I am so annoyed at someone else being the big noise. Two of a trade never agree.

Now what you want to get clear is that Pride is essentially competitive—is competitive by its very nature—while the other vices are competitive only, so to speak, by accident. Pride gets no pleasure out of having something, only out of having more of it than the next man. We say that people are proud of being rich, or clever, or good-looking, but they are not. They are proud of being richer, or cleverer, or better-looking than others. If everyone else became equally rich, or clever, or good-looking there would be nothing to be proud about. It is the comparison that makes you proud: the pleasure of being above the rest. Once the element of competition has gone, Pride has gone. That is why I say that Pride is essentially competitive in a way the other vices are not.

The sexual impulse may drive two men into competition if they both want the same girl. But that is only by accident; they might just as likely have wanted two different girls. But a proud man will take your girl from you, not because he wants her, but just to prove to himself that he is a better man than you.

121

Greed may drive men into competition if there is not enough to go round, but the proud man, even when he has got more than he can possibly want, will try to get still more just to assert his power. Nearly all those evils in the world which people put down to greed, or selfishness are really far more the result of Pride.

What makes a pretty girl spread misery wherever she goes by collecting admirers? Certainly not her sexual instinct: that kind of girl is quite often sexually frigid. It is Pride. . . .

Pride is competitive by its very nature; that is why it goes on and on. If I am a proud man, then, as long as there is one man in the whole world more powerful, or richer, or cleverer than I, he is my rival and my enemy.

The Christians are right; it is Pride which has been the chief cause of misery in every nation and every family since the world began. . . . But Pride always means enmity — it is enmity. And not only enmity between man and man, but enmity to God.

In God you come up against something which is in every respect immeasurably superior to yourself. Unless you know God as that — and, therefore, know yourself as nothing in comparison — you do not know God at all. As long as you are proud you cannot know God. A proud man is always looking down on things and people; and, of course, as long as you are looking down, you cannot see something that is above you.

That raises a terrible question. How is it that people who are quite obviously eaten up with Pride can say they believe in God and appear to themselves very religious? I am afraid it means they are worshiping an imaginary God. They theoretically admit themselves to be nothing in the presence of this phantom God, but are really all the time imagining how He approves of them and thinks them far better than ordinary people. . . . I suppose it was of those people Christ was thinking when He said that some would preach about Him and cast out devils in His name, only to be told at the end of the world that He had never known them. — C. S. Lewis in *Mere Christianity*.

Used by kind permission of Harper/Collins.

Nothing sets a person so much out of the devil's reach as humility. — Jonathan Edwards.

Mock Humility

Peter saith unto him, Thou shalt never wash my feet (John 13:8).

THOU shalt never wash my feet." This appears to be the expression of humility. How could Peter suffer that One so infinitely his superior should perform a service so menial? To many, perhaps, it may seem not only natural but every way fitting, that Peter should object to be thus waited upon by his Lord. This only shows, however, that to entertain a false conception of humility is something not peculiar to Peter.

For the sake of such, we remark, that whatever hinders us from receiving a blessing that God is willing to bestow upon us is not humility but the mockery of it. True humility will never betray the interests of the soul. That is not a true Christian grace which opposes the development of other Christian graces. By this test, try the spirits. Humility desires the utmost communication of God's favor, and anything that teaches you to decline the spiritual blessings that God is ready to bestow, know that it is of the earth, earthy.

So, on a previous occasion, Peter said, "Depart from me, O Lord, for I am a sinful man." Now, Satan would have desired above all things a compliance with this request. What shall we think, then, of the humility that dictated it? It is well to have conviction of sin—we cannot have it too deeply; we can scarcely take too dark a view of our own character—but humility, as a Christian grace, must ever draw the heart to Christ.

There is nothing more worthless than the self-deceit which leads some to say, "I am content to be an inferior Christian, and to be undistinguished by spiritual attainments; if I were a more devoted servant of the Lord, I might be lifted up with pride." That is to say, you, are afraid you would lose your humility if you obtained more faith. Well, lose your humility; it will be no great loss. If you really obtain a strong faith, you will have along with it a very different humility from that which you now have. Consider and confess. Your present humility is something most base, for it gives God the lie direct, saying it is not good for a man to love God with all his heart and soul, and further it says that He is not worthy that you should serve Him devotedly. It tears almost all the pages out of the Bible, for almost every page of Scripture contains promises, invitations, commands, which it nullifies.

A genuine humility will ever feel the need of the largest measures of grace, and will be perfected just in the degree in which that grace is bestowed. Spiritual pride shows, not that there has been too much, but too little, of the operation of the Spirit. The only way to overcome it is to press forward. The truly humble man will seek to be filled with all the fullness of God, knowing that when so filled there is not the slightest place for pride or for self. —George Bowen.

Andrew Bonar has voiced the same sentiments that George Bowen has just stated. "You need not be afraid," he assures us, "of too much grace. Great grace never makes a man proud. A little grace is very apt to make a man puffed up. Be afraid of a little grace. Great grace never puffs up."

Spiritual pride is a vice not only dreadfully mischievous in human society, but the most insuperable bar to real inward improvement. —E. Carter.

Who would have expected that spiritual pastors would be warned against lordliness and pride? Who would have imagined that men who are ministering the Gospel of lowliness should themselves be exalted in pride! It is one of the most insidious temptations which besets the working disciple of Christ. Pride ever lurks just at the heels of power. Even a little authority is prone to turn the seemly walk into a most offensive strut. —J. H. Jowett in *The First Epistle of Peter.*

Boasting or Belittling

Where is boasting then? It is excluded. By what law? of works? Nay: but by the law of faith (Rom. 3:27).

WE all know how painful it is to be forced to listen to a confirmed boaster sound off on his favorite topic — himself. To be the captive of such a man even for a short time tries our patience to the utmost and puts a heavy strain upon our Christian charity. Boasting is particularly offensive when it is heard among the children of God, the one place above all others where it should never be found. Yet it is quite common among Christians, though usually disguised somewhat by the use of the stock expression, "I say this to the glory of God. . . ."

Another habit not quite so odious is belittling ourselves. This might seem to be the exact opposite of boasting, but actually, it is the same old sin traveling under a *nom de plume*. It is simply egoism trying to act spiritual. It is impatient Saul hastily offering an unacceptable sacrifice to the Lord. Self-derogation is bad for the reason that self must be there to derogate. Self, whether swaggering or groveling, can never be anything but hateful to God.

Boasting is an evidence that we are pleased with self, and belittling that we are disappointed in it. Either way we reveal that we have a high opinion of ourselves. The belittler is chagrined that one as obviously superior as he should not have done better, and he punishes himself by making uncomplimentary remarks about himself. That he does not really mean what he says may be proved quite easily. Let someone else say the same things. His eager defence of himself will reveal how he feels and has secretly felt all the time.

The victorious Christian neither exalts nor downgrades himself. His interests have shifted from self to Christ. What he is or is not no longer concerns him. He believes that he has been crucified with Christ and he is not willing either to praise or deprecate such a man.

Yet the knowledge that he has been crucified is only half the victory. "Nevertheless I live; yet not I, but Christ liveth in me: and the life which I now live in the flesh I live by the faith of the Son of God, who loved me, and gave himself for me." Christ is now where the man's ego was formerly. The man is now Christ-centered instead of self-centered, and he forgets himself in his delighted preoccupation with Christ.

Candor compels me to acknowledge that it is a lot easier to write about this than it is to live it. Self is one of the toughest plants that grows in the garden of life. It is, in fact, indestructible by any human means. Just when we are sure it is dead it turns up somewhere as robust as ever to trouble our peace and poison the fruit of our lives.

Yet there is deliverance. When our judicial crucifixion becomes actual the victory is near, and when our faith rises to claim the risen life of Christ as our own the triumph is complete. The trouble is that we do not receive the benefits of all this until something radical has happened in our own experience, something which in its psychological effects approaches actual crucifixion. What Christ went through we also must go through. Rejection, surrender, loss, a violent detachment from the world, the pain of social ostracism — all must be felt in our actual experience. . . .

While we boast or belittle we may be perfectly sure that the cross has not yet done its work within us. Faith and obedience will bring the cross into the life and cure both habits. — A. W. Tozer, in *Man The Dwelling Place of God.*

Children are often able to express great truths most simply. Some youngsters had formed a club and put up rules. The first rule was worded thus: "Nobody act big, nobody act small, everybody act medium."

Boasting is always an advertisement of poverty.
— W. Graham Scroggie.

The Detestable Vanity

Hezekiah rendered not again according to the benefit done unto him; for his heart was lifted up: therefore there was wrath upon him... (2 Chron. 32:25). But when he was strong, his heart was lifted up to his destruction... (2 Chron. 26:16).

IN the Old Testament, we have two examples of spiritual pride. In the case of both Hezekiah and Uzziah, pride ruined their otherwise good record. They had been zealous for the Lord's honor until they became strong and then pride, that most insidious of all sins, took possession of their hearts, thus bringing God's wrath upon them.

Even since her early days, the Church has ever been troubled by self-seeking ministers. Basil, a Church Father of the fourth century, inveighs against this form of wickedness in high places: "Everyone is a theologian, even he whose life is stained with countless pollutions. Self-appointed individuals with a keen appetite for place reject the dispensation of the Holy Spirit, and then divide among themselves the high offices of the Church. There is an indescribable pushing and elbowing for precedence, every one who is eager to make an appearance straining every nerve to put himself forward prominently."

An entry in the dairy of Oswald Chambers reads like this: "Mr. Swan was addressing some Christian Effendis and called me over to tell them what I considered the real danger of theological training. I promptly said, 'Swelled head,' and explained my belief that the only way to maintain spiritual life along with intellectual life was by the submission of the intellect to Jesus Christ, and that then intellect became a splendid handmaiden of the Lord; that intellect should be the feet and not the head of the student. I gave them Philippians 3:10."

Dr. Upham, Madam Guyon's biographer and a very useful minister who advocated a holy life, warned: "Where there is true Christian perfection, there is always great humility — a Christian grace which it is difficult to define, but which implies at least a quiet and subdued, a meek and forbearing spirit. Whatever may be our supposed gifts, whatever may be our internal pleasures and raptures, they are far from furnishing evidence of completeness of Christian character without humility. It is this grace which, perhaps more than any other, imparts a beauty and attractiveness to the religious life."

Samuel Pearse was called the Brainerd of the Baptists and did much to forward the missionary enterprise of William Carey in India by faithfully "holding the ropes" at home. Later, his daughter married one of Dr. Carey's sons. Pearse was aware of his danger to spiritual pride as is recorded by his biographer: "'I am ashamed,' he writes to Ryland, 'that I have so much pride. I want more and more to become a little child, to dwindle into nothing in my esteem, to renounce my own wisdom, power, and goodness, and to simply live upon Jesus for all.'

"In a letter to his wife from Plymouth he sadly confesses: 'My thirst for preaching Christ, I fear, abates; and a detestable vanity for the reputation of a good preacher, as the world terms it, has already cost me many conflicts.'

"Probably in Plymouth there were many kinsfolk to glory in his greatening powers, and to offer the perilous praises. To Carey he writes: 'Flattering prospects of reputation and wealth have had too much ascendancy over me.'"

Humility is but another name for the spirit of dependence. It is the realization of our true condition before God. The world's humility is mere diffidence or fear or affectation, but real humility is truth and confidence and assured hope; for the truly humble heart recognizes itself as a receiver, and feels content to be so. It hears its Lord telling it to open its mouth wide, and it knows that grace will assuredly be given and that abundantly. — Thomas Erskine.

Stealing the Glory

Let the LORD be magnified (Psa. 35:27).
No flesh should glory in his presence (1 Cor. 1:29).

REVIVAL tarries because we steal the glory that belongs to God. Listen to this and wonder: Jesus said, "I receive not honour from men," and, "How can ye believe, which receive honour one of another, and seek not the honour that cometh from God only?" (John 5:41,44). Away with all fleshly back-slapping and platform flattery! Away with this exalting of "My radio program," "My church," "My books!" Oh, the sickening parade of flesh in our pulpits; "We are greatly privileged, etc." Speakers (who are there really by grace alone) accept all this, nay — even expect it! The fact is that when we have listened to most of these men, we would not have known that they were great if they had not been announced so!

POOR GOD! He does not get much out of it all! Then why doesn't God fulfil His blessed and yet awful promise and spew us out of His mouth? We have failed. We are filthy. We love men's praise. We "seek our own." "Oh God, lift us out of this rut and this rot! Bless us with breakings! Judgment must begin with us preachers!" —Leonard Ravenhill, in *Why Revival Tarries.*

Henry Moorehouse was a young minister who proved a blessing to D. L. Moody for he was literally drenched in the Word of God. On one occasion, Moody had to go away for a week and so asked for this minister to preach for him. Upon returning home, he asked how the services were going. Upon being told that he had preached each night on John 3:16, Moody was surprised that any preacher could find enough material to hold an audience night after night upon the same verse. But when he went to hear for himself, he was strangely moved, and became a closer reader of the Word as a result.

The secret of his effective preaching is shown in the following incident: "Henry Moorehouse, while still a young man, was conducting evangelistic services in a certain city in this country, but there was no revival. God had given him precious revivals both in America and in Great Britain, but in this city it was as though he was up against a stone wall. Day and night he was on his knees, searching his heart and crying out, 'O God, why is there no revival?'

"One day as he was walking along the street, the Holy Spirit showed him a large placard on which appeared these words: 'Henry Moorehouse, The Most Famous of all British Preachers!' At once he said to himself, 'That's why there is no revival!' He went at once to the campaign committee and said, 'Brethren, now I know why there is no revival. See how you have advertised me as the greatest of this and the greatest of that! No wonder the Holy Spirit cannot work! He is grieved and quenched because you haven't magnified the Lord Jesus Christ. He is the wonderful One. I'm just a poor, simple, humble servant, preaching the glorious Gospel."

—*Herald of His Coming.*

O thou unpolished shaft, why leave the quiver?
    O thou blunt axe, what forests canst thou hew?
Untempered sword, canst thou the oppressed deliver?
    Go back to thine own Maker's forge anew.

Submit thyself to God for preparation,
    Seek not to teach thy Master and thy Lord;
Call it not zeal; it is a base temptation.
    Satan is pleased when man dictates to God.

Down with thy pride! With holy vengeance trample
    On each self-flattering fancy that appears;
Did not the Lord Himself, for our example,
    Lie hid in Nazareth for thirty years?
—Unknown.

The Tragedy of Strife in the Church

Let nothing be done through strife or vainglory; but in lowliness of mind let each esteem other better than themselves (Phil. 2:3).

THE lust for power burns in the Christian worker. Ambition for personal victory possesses the heart of the professed soldier of the Cross. The spirit of strife enters into the messenger of peace. Men do Christian work because impelled by strife. Men persist in Christian service because impelled by vain-glory. Strife and vain-glory, the powers of the world, become motive powers in the Kingdom of God. That is the pity of it, and the tragedy of it, that a kingdom purposed for the destruction of self can be used for the fattening of self — a kingdom established for the annihilation of worldliness used for its enthronement.

"The gist of the whole matter is this: it is possible to make a worldly convenience of the Christ, to regard Him as an agent in the attainment of mere party ends, and to use Him with a single eye for our own glory. It is against this insidious and imminent peril that the Apostle warns us when he counsels us, in all the varied work of the Church, to 'let nothing be done through strife or vain-glory.'

"What we have before us is a warning against the obtrusion of self in Christian service. Now the Apostle says that this obtrusion may reveal itself in one of two shapes: in strife or vain-glory. I think it will be well, in the place of both these words, to substitute more modern equivalents which will enable us to catch the Apostle's thought. What did the Apostle mean by strife? Party-spirit. What did he mean by vain-glory? Personal vanity. 'Let nothing be done through party-spirit or personal vanity.' Party-spirit! Personal vanity! Those are the two guises in which self is apt to intrude into Church life and crowd out the Christ. . . .

"Party-spirit is that which seeks the luxury of a majority more than the enthronement of a truth. It aims at winning a contest rather than at advancing a cause. It works for sectarian triumph more than for spiritual growth. . . . Party-spirit is in the Church when the Christian fights harder for a sectarian triumph than for the reign of the Lord. There are some members of the Christian Church who are never to be found in the battlefield except when the struggle is an unfortunate contest between the Christian sects. . . .

"Personal vanity! A man can be a sect to himself; he can be a party of one. He can seek his own triumphs, his own majorities. Such a man begins counting everything from himself, but the tragedy is that a man who begins by counting himself as 'number one' never gets as far as 'number two'; with 'number one' the numeration ends. Personal vanity — a life swollen with pride. The eyes are so 'enclosed in fat' that 'number two' is never seen. Personal vanity — that is the obtrusion we have to fear and beware.

"The Apostle declares that this spirit of personal vanity may obtrude into the Church. Nay, he declares that men and women will come into the Church in order to feed it. They will use the holy ministries of the Church to fatten self. We can bow our heads to pray through sheer personal vanity. We can engage in services of philanthropy through sheer personal vanity. We can preach Christ crucified through sheer personal vanity. That is stern, hard, and horrible, not as fiction but as fact, and we shall do well to face it. I can be in the Church of Christ like a huge sponge, a mere agent of suction, gathering and retaining solely to increase the weight of self."

—J. H. Jowett in *Brooks by the Traveller's Way.*

When I survey the wondrous cross
  On which the Prince of glory died,
My richest gain I count but loss,
  And pour contempt on all my pride.
               —Isaac Watts.

False Glory

That ye may have somewhat to answer them which glory in appearance, and not in heart (2 Cor. 5:12).
The LORD seeth not as man seeth; for man looketh on the outward appearance, but the Lord looketh on the heart (1 Sam. 16:7).

HUMILITY is closely linked to simplicity and sincerity. Before we can enter into the Kingdom of God, we must appear as we really are—naked and bare—in the sight of God. This unveiling of our true condition is humiliating, and we can never quite be the same afterwards. The desire, however, to cover up by an outward exterior is innate in man. He knows what will enhance his reputation. Even Samuel, when choosing a king, had to be reproved for looking on the countenance and stature of the candidates. He was only too aware of what we would call "electability" which is generally based on personal charisma, education, and wealth.

The eighth chapter of 1 Samuel relates a serious crisis in the history of Israel. God had elected the Israelites as His witnesses to show the heathen nations around them how superior was the Captain of their armies—the invisible God—Who was not interested in the strength of the horse or the legs of a man. He reproved their motives in wishing to be like the surrounding nations. If they were to have a king, their trust would be in chariots and horses which had been forbidden to the Israelites; they would build palaces, have large standing armies and impressive armaments. Theirs would be a false glory.

We see this tragically illustrated in Solomon; he reached the height of outward grandeur, but moral decay had set in. The people were heavily taxed, and they cried out because of it after Solomon died. Jesus contrasted the outward glory of Solomon with the beautiful lily whose goodness came from within. "Solomon in all his glory was not arrayed like one of these." Excessive outward array betrays inward emptiness.

When Christianity had most spiritual power her buildings were simple. Today, church buildings cost millions, their luxury often being highly mortgaged. The choice of a minister depends upon the demands of carnal members for someone who will attract the world to their church. The humble Carpenter of Nazareth would disdain the splendor that is our false glory, and would be totally unacceptable in many of our pulpits.

This dependence upon outward appearances began to harass the Church, even in her infancy. An early Church Father, Chrysostom, said: "And what then is modest apparel? Such as covers them completely and decently and not with superfluous ornaments; for the one is decent and the other is not. What? Do you approach God to pray with broidered hair and ornaments of gold? Are you come to a ball, to a marriage feast, to a carnival? There such costly things might have been seasonable . . . here not one of them is wanted. You are come to pray, to ask pardon for your sins, to plead for your offences, beseeching the Lord, and hoping to render Him propitious to you. Away with such hypocrisy! God is not mocked. This is the attire of actors and dancers, who live upon the stage. Nothing of this kind becomes a modest woman who should be adorned with shamefacedness and sobriety."

Many centuries later, John Wesley bemoaned the increasing finery of his people, the Methodists. Finney changed his views on the subject considerably, saying, "I will confess that I was formerly myself in error. I believed that the best way for Christians to pursue was to dress so as not to be noticed, to follow the fashions so as not to be noticed, to follow the fashions so as not to appear singular. But I have seen my error and now wonder greatly at my former blindness. It is your duty to dress so plain as to show the world that you place no sort of reliance in things of fashion."

Soon Christ will return in splendor and true glory for those who have refused to bow to the peer pressures of ungodly men and women and have chosen the way of the Cross. — Lillian Harvey.

Pride of Dress

Whose adorning let it not be that outward adorning . . . But let it be the hidden man of the heart . . . even the ornament of a meek and quiet spirit. . . . For after this manner in the old time the holy women also . . . adorned themselves. . . (1 Peter 3:3-5).

THIS book would not be complete without the mention of another form of pride which is particularly prevalent among those who, only too often, submit to the dictates of fashion rather than conform to the Word of God. Whenever God has come near in reviving power, there has always been deep conviction, particularly among women, for this pride of dress. They become aware of possessing motives to display their persons and thus compete with their sisters whose disdain they wish to avoid.

John Fletcher did not allow this form of pride to go unnoticed. Let us quote his own words: "I cannot pass in silence the detestable though fashionable sin which has brought down the curse of Heaven, and poured desolation and ruin upon the most flourishing kingdoms—I mean pride in apparel. Even in this place where poverty, hard labor, and drudgery would, one should think, prevent a sin which Christianity cannot tolerate even in king's houses, there are not wanting foolish virgins who draw iniquity with cords of vanity, and betray the levity of their hearts by that of their dress.

"Yes, some women, who should be mothers in Israel, and adorn themselves with good works as holy and godly matrons, openly affect the opposite character. You may see them offer themselves first to the idol of vanity, and then sacrifice their children upon the same altar. As some sons of Belial teach their little ones to curse before they can well speak, so these daughters of Jezebel drag their unhappy offspring before they can walk to the haunts of vanity and pride. They complain of evening lectures, but run to midnight dancings. Oh, that such persons would let the prophet's words sink into their frothy minds, and fasten upon their careless hearts: 'Because the daughters of Sion are haughty and walk with stretched-forth necks and wanton eyes, the Lord will smite with a sore the crown of their head, and discover their shame: instead of well-set hair, there shall be baldness, and burning instead of beauty.'"

Mary Bosanquet, who later married John Fletcher, was from a most fashion-loving home circle where persons of great worldly honor were often entertained. When Mary experienced the convicting power of the Holy Spirit, she obeyed God and was disinherited as a result. She doubtless had to listen to covert accusations of legality and bondage which often scare many women from their humble walk. But Mary Fletcher was well aware of the benefits of her unworldly attire as is revealed in the following quotation:

"I saw clearly that plainness of dress and behavior best became a Christian. The Apostle expressly forbids women professing godliness to let their adorning be in apparel, allowing them no other ornament than that of a 'meek and quiet spirit.'

"It (plainness of dress) tended to open my mouth; for when I appeared like the women of the world in Babylonish garments, I had its esteem, and knew not how to part with it. But when I showed by my appearance that I considered myself as a stranger and foreigner, none can know, but by trying, what an influence it has on our whole conduct, and what a fence it is to keep us from sinking into the spirit of the world. For there is no medium; they who are conformed to the fashions, customs and maxims of the world, must embrace the spirit also, and they shall find the esteem they seek, for the world will love its own. But let them remember also that word, 'The friendship of the world is enmity with God.'"

— *The Life of Mary Fletcher.*

High Living and Hell

Son, remember that thou in thy lifetime receivedst thy good things, and likewise Lazarus evil things: but now he is comforted, and thou art tormented (Luke 16:25).

L EONARD Ravenhill in his most searching book, *Why Revival Tarries*, lists his reasons for spiritual dearth; one such reason is the extravagant living of the would-be promoters of revival. We quote from his book:

"The tithes of widows and of the poor are spent in luxury-living by many evangelists. The great crowds, great lines of seekers, great appreciation by the mayor, etc., are shouted to high heaven. All get publicity — except the love offering! The poor dupes who give, 'think they do God service,' while all they are doing is keeping a big-reputationed, small-hearted preacher living in Hollywood style.

"Preachers who have homes and cottages by the lake, a boat on that lake, and a big bank balance, still beg for more. With such extortioners and unjust men, can God entrust Holy Ghost revival? These dear, doll-like preacher-boys no longer change their suits once a day, but two or three times a day. They preach the Jesus of the stable, but themselves live in swank hotels. For their own lusts they bleed the audience financially in the name of the One Who had to borrow a penny to illustrate His sermon. They wear expensive Hollywood suits in honor of One Who wore a peasant's robe. They feast on three-dollar steaks in remembrance of the One Who fasted alone in the desert. Today an evangelist is not only worthy of his hire (so he thinks), but of compound interest. How fearful will all this be in the judgment morning!"

Elizabeth Forster was a Mildmay deaconess living most simply and humbly for God. She married Michael Baxter and together they edited *The Christian Herald* and *The Life of Faith*, not to mention the many books that Marshall, Morgan, and Scott published. We quote from one of the many articles which she wrote for these periodicals:

"But faith in Jesus Christ has never been and never will be a popular thing. The humility of His birth, the obscurity of His early days, the plebeian occupation of the Carpenter of Nazareth, all spoke of the 'dry ground,' and reflected no credit upon the grandeur of that human nature, of which men who do not understand God can boast themselves.

"Human nature always seeks its own, sets a value upon itself, wills to be self-dependent, and measures all others by its overvalued self. No wonder then that 'He was despised and rejected of men. . . .'

"Men cannot understand a hidden life. They press every advantage to make as much of themselves as they can. But here was something more than modesty in Jesus: He hid His face that He might manifest His Father's; He sank into insignificance that He might be the express Image of His Father, so serving His purpose in everything. This is the way of the Cross for us as for our Master.

"The way of the cross not only saves man from Hell, but also crosses him out, to write the name of Jesus Christ in the place of his; Christ hides man and manifests God."

> Jesus, I my cross have taken,
>   All to leave and follow Thee;
> Destitute, despised, forsaken,
>   Thou from hence mine all shalt be.
>
> Perish ev'ry fond ambition,
>   All I've sought, and hoped, and known:
> Yet how rich is my condition!
>   God and Heav'n are still mine own.
>   —Henry F. Lyte.

We Are Nothing

For if a man think himself to be something, when he is nothing, he deceiveth himself (Gal. 6:3).

THE above verse was made very real to me some years ago. I had always thought it was a reproof to certain Galatians, but I later saw that it was a statement of fact. *We are nothing*, and to think ourselves something when we are not is ridiculous. But pride blinds the eyes to our true state until the revelation of Jesus enlightens us.

We were not creators but His creation. We are but zeroes in the great world of spiritual mathematics. The zero, however, is very vital if we wish to increase the value of a numeral. Each zero placed after the numeral increases its worth tenfold until we reach the millions, billions, trillions, and so on. Christ is the numeral. We are the zeroes. "All things were made by him; and without him was not anything made that was made." A tremendous truth! When we fell in Adam, we wished to be the creators, the originators, the numerals. But we are nothing, so the Bible states again and again.

If we place the zero in front of the numeral, we decrease its value tenfold. It becomes a mere fraction, and the more zeroes we place before the numeral, the less its value becomes. On the Day of Pentecost, one hundred and twenty zeroes lined up after the Christ, and they shook Jerusalem. How many today who profess His name, foolishly put themselves in front of Christ, thus lessening His value in the world's eyes without increasing their own value one whit!

"He must increase, but I must decrease," said the lowly John the Baptist who was filled with the Holy Ghost from his mother's womb (John 3:30). All through his short history, we find that he had a true estimate of both himself and of the Christ. He described the Messiah to those who flocked to hear him, saying, "He that cometh after me is preferred before me: for he was before me." This he said three times in the first chapter of his Gospel. In John 1:15,27, & 30, we find him making this same statement — "He is preferred before me."

One coming in time after him, nevertheless, was before him. The numeral was before the nothing. John enhanced the value of Christ saying that he, himself, was but a voice in the wilderness, and yet he was so popular at one time that he could easily have placed himself before the Christ. But "one cometh before me," he said. He saw by the aid of the Spirit's illumination that Christ, although born after him in "time," had existed all through eternity.

Oh, that we had the insight which John had! Our brief span of life is our opportunity to exalt Christ by placing Him before ourselves, that He might increase and we decrease. Our task is ever after to "follow," "follow," "follow." "Follow me and I will make you fishers of men." A disciple is one who follows, hence the word "followers."

Paul took that judicial sentence of death in himself, that he should not trust in himself, but in Christ. He said to those who listened to him in the early Church, "Follow me, but only as you find me following Christ." He came after. Will we come after? Will we cease trying to be something when we are nothing? — Lillian Harvey.

Where is the man who would not like to be something, be it in nature or in the spirit? But this arrogance, that we each one want to be something, is the root of evil. It is the cause that we are so often displeased with God and men and live without peace and without grace. With a willing and thankful heart we must accept it if someone leads us to see our own nothingness; as long as a single drop of blood in us has not died we cannot truly say with Paul, "I live, yet not I, but Christ liveth in me." He who wants to be something for God must have ceased to live to himself and to be something in himself. For of ourselves we are nothing, we are something only in Him. — Heinrich Suso.

He Takes Things Which Are Not

But God hath chosen . . . things which are not, to bring to nought things that are: That no flesh should glory in his presence (1 Cor. 1:27-29).

WHEN man launches a new enterprise, he generally does so in a big way — famous speakers, big advertisements, and wealthy patrons. When God launched His Gospel of the Kingdom, He chose the things which are not to bring to naught the things that are. Why? So that no man might glory in His presence.

Let us see how this emphasis on nothingness is demonstrated to us throughout the Bible:

The Nothing of Goodness. The sinner does not receive regenerating grace until he comes with nothing in his hands. When the men in debt had nothing to pay, he frankly forgave them both. When the prodigal came to the end of his resources, he was ready for the Father's embracing acceptance. No work of righteousness could ever enhance the finished work of Calvary. This is illustrated in the following Scriptures:

1. "When they had nothing to pay, he frankly forgave them both" (Luke 7:42).

2. "When he had spent all, there arose a mighty famine in that land; and he began to be in want. . . . He said . . . I perish with hunger" (Luke 15:14,17).

The Nothing of Strength. The healing virtue of Jesus flowed out to those who had become conscious of their strengthlessness. "They that are whole need not a physician." The full He sent empty away; but it was to the hungry and the thirsty, that He dealt out the Bread of Life. So when we have tried earth's resources and are nothing bettered, then He comes with His healing virtue. Again, we have illustrations of this principle throughout the New Testament:

141

1. "A certain woman . . . had suffered many things . . . and had spent all that she had, and was nothing bettered, but rather grew worse" (Mark 5:25,26).

2. "The impotent man answered him, Sir, I have no man, when the water is troubled, to put me into the pool" (John 5:7).
— Lillian Harvey.

St. Francis of Assisi was one time asked how he could accomplish what he did. He replied: "This may be why. The Lord looked down from Heaven and said, 'Where can I find the weakest, littlest, meanest man on earth?' When He saw me He said, 'I found him; he won't be proud of it; he'll see that I am using him because of his insignificance.'"

The humble man of God has a curious sense of powerlessness. I have often thought God looked all the world over to find a man weak enough to do the work. — Bishop Montgomery.

Mark the fact that the Lord uses instruments that are remarkable for their weakness. — J. G. Gregory.

> O to be nothing, nothing,
>   Only to lie at His feet,
> A broken and emptied vessel,
>   For the Master's use made meet.
>
> Emptied, that He might fill me,
>   As forth to His service I go;
> Broken, that so, unhindered,
>   His life through me might flow.
>
> O! to be nothing, nothing,
>   Painful the humbling may be;
> Yet low in the dust I'd lay me
>   That the world my Savior might see.
> — Unknown.

He Uses Nothings

It is the spirit that quickeneth; the flesh profiteth nothing (John 6:63).
I can of mine own self do nothing (John 5:30).

IN the previous reading, we noticed several important "nothings" of Scripture. Here are a few more which are well worth our consideration:

The Nothing of Resources. It was to those who had toiled all night and caught nothing that Christ gave the secret for a successful catch. It was the empty larder, the empty vessels, the multitude without sustenance — all provided a platform for God's bountiful giving, as is shown in the following verses:

1. "I have nothing to set before him" (Luke 11:6).

2. "They have nothing to eat" (Matt. 15:32).

3. "They have no wine" (John 2:3).

4. "Silver and gold have I none; but such as I have give I thee" (Acts 3:6).

5. "I have not a cake, but an handful of meal in a barrel, and a little oil in a cruse: and, behold, I am gathering two sticks, that I may go in and dress it for me and my son, that we may eat it, and die" (1 Kings 17: 12).

6. "Go, borrow thee vessels abroad of all thy neighbors, even empty vessels; borrow not a few" (2 Kings 4:3).

In these Old Testament stories we have the same principle exemplified. The widow has enough for one more meal, and yet she gives to the prophet. A widow's debt brought her into dire circumstances. Elisha came on the scene and told her to secure empty vessels, not a few. The supply was determined by the number of empty vessels.

The Nothing of Success. It is not the lazy worker that discovers the miraculous powers of Christ. It is the one who has toiled all night and taken nothing, who sees Christ on the shore of his life. Listening, he hears the words of authority and lets down the empty nets of his vain endeavors, and the net is full of fish. "We have toiled all the night, and have taken nothing" (Luke 5:5).

The Nothing of Reward. "Do good, and lend, hoping for nothing again; and your reward shall be great" (Luke 6:35). What a test for selfish money hoarders! How contrary to the world's view of giving and lending!

"For we brought nothing into this world, and it is certain we can carry nothing out" (1 Tim. 6:7). It is said that John Wesley "told someone that if at his death he had more than ten pounds ($23.00) in his possession, people had the privilege of calling him a robber. Near the end of his life he wrote in his journal very simply, 'I left no money to anyone in my will because I had none.'"

We start as nothings, and we should, if we have wisely obeyed God with our substance, leave nothing. How many family squabbles and lawsuits have resulted from unfaithful stewardship. Money that could have been distributed wisely to the needy and to God's missionary enterprises is left too often to worldly sons and daughters. This often proves their ruin. —Lillian Harvey.

Our all, O God, is nothing in Thine eyes,
    Our nothing Thou regardest oft with love;
Glory and pomp of words Thou dost not prize,
    Thy impulse only gives them power to move.
Thy noblest works awaken not man's praise,
    For they are hidden, and he blindly turns
Away, nor though he see, their light discerns;
    Too gross his sense, too keen their dazzling rays.
          —Unknown.

The founder of the Brethren movement, J. N. Darby, seemed to understand much concerning God's ways of working. "Oh, the joy of having nothing," he once exclaimed, "and being nothing, seeing nothing but a living Christ in glory, and being careful for nothing but His interest down here."

I Failed, He Conquered

A man's heart deviseth his way: but the Lord directeth his steps (Prov. 16:9).

IN 1798, Alfred Barnes was born in Rome, New York. His father was a mechanic. At school, he showed good talents, and his father at length consented that he might attempt to get a liberal education. His heart was set on the law, but God made him a minister, turned his thoughts toward the Holy Scriptures as a field of study, and before he died at the age of seventy-two years, a million volumes of his Biblical Commentaries had been sold.

William Plummer tells us more of this remarkable man: "Now did he do all these things of his own power and wisdom? Not at all. Hear his modest and truthful statement on the subject: 'I have carried out none of the purposes of my early years. I have failed in those things which I had designed, and which I hoped to accomplish. I have done what I never purposed or expected to do. I have known what it was to weep at discouragements. I have been led along contrary to my early anticipations. I can now see, I think, that while I have been conscious of entire freedom in all that I have done, yet that my whole life has been under the absolute control of a Higher Power, and that there has been a will and a plan in regard to my life which was not my own. Even my most voluntary acts, I can see, have been subservient to that higher plan, and what I have done has been done as if I had no agency in the matter.'

"These things being so, we should never forget:

"(1). That it is our duty to remember all the way the Lord our God has led us. Whatever of comfort or success has attended our labors, was the fruit of His kindness and wisdom and power. Man is as feeble as he is foolish, as sinful as he is helpless. His wisdom is folly. He is crushed before the moth. Only by the Lord can we do valiantly; only by Him can we have good success. By Him David leaped over a wall; by Him David broke through a host; by Him David slew Goliath.

"(2). The Lord is Governor. He manages all things. 'Man proposes, God disposes.' God's providence and His Word doth declare, 'The way of man is not in himself: it is not in man that walketh to direct his steps'; 'A man's heart deviseth his way: but the Lord directeth his steps'; 'There are many devices in a man's heart; nevertheless the counsel of the Lord, that shall stand.' Such is the uniform tenor of thought in God's Word.

"(3). If our success depends entirely upon God, let us look constantly to Him and trust Him, watch His providence, keep His commandments, and live for His glory. Woe to him that striveth with his Maker! The Lord is never successfully opposed."

I asked of God that He should give success
  To the high task I sought for Him to do;
I asked that every hindrance might grow less
  And that my hours of weakness might be few;
    I asked that far and lofty heights be scaled;
    And now I humbly thank Him that I failed.

For with the pain and sorrow came to me
  A dower of tenderness in act and thought;
And with the failure came a sympathy,
  An insight which success had never brought.
    Father, I had been foolish and unblest
    If Thou hadst granted me my blind request.
                              —J. Stuart Holden.

"Beyond controversy, humility is indispensable to the true life of the soul," says H. P. Liddon. "There are graces which may be given or withheld; experiences, assurances, raptures, ecstasies. But no man ever went to Heaven without learning humility on this side of the grave.

"Without humility religious progress is impossible. The true growth of the soul is not to be measured by our attempting many extraordinary duties but by our power of doing simple duties well. And humility, when it reigns in the soul, carries this principle into practice. It bids us hallow our work, especially whatever may be to us hard or distasteful work."

146

Insufficient – All Sufficient

Not that we are sufficient of ourselves. . . . Our sufficiency is of God; Who also hath made us able ministers (2 Cor. 3:5, 6).

IN a crisis hour of my spiritual experience," said A. B. Simpson, founder of the Christian Missionary Alliance, "while asking counsel from an old, experienced friend, I was shocked to receive this answer, 'All you need in order to bring you into the blessing you are seeking and to make your life a power for God, is to be annihilated.' The fact is, the shock of that message almost annihilated me for the time, but before God's faithful discipline was through, I had learned in some adequate measure, as I have been learning ever since, the great truth, 'I am not sufficient to think anything of myself.'

"Once in my early ministry I traveled a thousand miles to go to one of Mr. Moody's conventions of ministers in Chicago. I reached there about six o'clock in the evening and went up to the early meeting. I did not hear Mr. Moody say anything, but one plain, earnest preacher got up with his face all shining. He said, 'I came up here expecting Mr. Moody to help me. But last night I saw Jesus, and I got such a look at Jesus that I am never going to need anything again as long as I live.' And he wound up with a long Hallelujah. Something smote my heart. 'All you need is Jesus; you go to Him.' I took the train back home that night. I did not wait for the convention. I went to my office in the church vestry, and I waited there on my face at His blessed feet until He came, and thank God, He enabled me in some measure to say, 'I have seen Jesus, and my wants are all supplied.'"

Through reading the writings of this saintly man we come to see how fully he grasped God's teaching of man's nothingness so that he might trust the inexhaustible resources of grace. Speaking of Moses, he writes:

147

"When God gets him there, reduced to the smallest of proportions, the weakest of all men that ever lived, He says, 'You are ready for work; now, Moses, I am going to take that rod and with it break the arms of Pharaoh and open the way for My people, and bring waters from the desert rock, and make you an instrument of power.'" — *Divine Emblems.*

As someone who had become thoroughly acquainted with his own utter dependence on Christ for everything, A.B. Simpson was able to define humility thus:

"He who seeks not his own interest, but solely God's interest in time and eternity, he is humble.... Many study exterior humility, but humility which does not flow from love is spurious. The more this exterior humility stoops, the loftier it inwardly feels itself, but he who is conscious of stooping does not really feel himself to be so low that he can go no further.

"People who think much of their humility are very proud.... Many men seeking to be humble by an effort of their will, and failing in perfect resignation and self-renunciation, sin against the Divine love without which there is no humility. Fuller light would enable them to see that they are exalting themselves by that which they mean for humility — their supposed setting aside of self is self-seeking; they are puffed up with the pride of humility and glory in the humble acts they perform.

"But the really humble man does not do anything of the sort; he lets himself be carried hither and thither; he is satisfied that God should do as He will with him, as the wind with the straw, and there is more humility in accepting greatness in such a spirit than in thwarting God's plans beneath a pretext of humility. He who chooses abasement rather than elevation is not necessarily humble, though he may wish to be; but he who lets himself go up or down, heedless whether to be praised or blamed, unmindful of what is said of him, is really humble, whatever men may think, if it be because he waits solely on God's pleasure." — *Emblems of the Holy Spirit.*

Mastered by God

Humble yourselves in the sight of the Lord, and he shall lift you up (James 4:10).

THIS reading is by P. T. Forsyth, that most provocative of writers, who brings to our attention a still different aspect of humility:

"Humility is a great mystery to itself. It is the amazement of the redeemed soul before itself, or rather before Christ in itself. It may take the shape of modesty before men, or it may not; humility is not anything which we have in the sight or thought of other men at all. It is the soul's attitude before God.... It can take very active, assertive, and even fiery shape in dealing with men. It is not timidity or nervousness. It is not shy, not embarrassed, not hesitant, not self-conscious, not ill at ease, not a seeker of back seats or mien of low shoulders and drooping head. Yet it is not self-sufficient in a proud and Stoic reserve, nor self-assertive in a public Pharisee fashion. It can never be had either by imitating the humble or by mortifying the flesh. Devotion is not humility, though humility is devout. It is only to be had by the mastery of the Cross which taketh away the self-wrapped guilt of the world.

"With humility goes patience as a supreme confession of faith. Do not think that patience is a way of bearing trouble only. It is a way of doing work—especially the true secret of not doing too much work. It is a way of carrying success. It is not renouncing will and becoming careless. It is an act of will. It is a piece of manhood. To part with will is to become a *thing*. It is not mere resignation or indifference, which often goes with despair and not faith. It is a form of energy, even when it curbs energy. It is the Christian form of bravery, and it has the valor often to be called cowardice. It is the form of energy that converts suffering, and even helplessness, into action. . . .

"It is not very often, comparatively, that the New Testament writers offer Christ as our example. But when they do, it is almost always in connection with His humility and patience and self-sacrificing love. It is His spirit, His faith and love, that are our example, not His conduct, not His way of life.

"Humility is a frame of perfect mind not possible except to faith. It is no more depression and poverty of spirit than it is loud self-depreciation. It rests on our deep sense of God's unspeakable gift, on a deep sense of our sin as mastered by God, on a deep sense of the Cross as the power which won that victory. It is not possible where the central value of the Cross is forgotten, where the Cross is only the glorification of self-sacrifice instead of the atonement for sin. A faith that lives outside the atonement must lose humility, as so much Christian faith in a day like this has lost it, as so much worship has lost awe.

"It is very hard, unless we are really and inly broken with Christ on the Cross, to keep from making our self the center and measure of all the world. This happens even in our well-doing. We may escape from selfishness, but it is hard to escape from a subtle egotism which it is not quite fair to call selfish. This personal masterfulness of ours needs mastering. In many respects it is very useful, but it must go ere God in Christ is done with us. And it is mastered only by the Cross as the one atonement for sin." — *Christian Perfection*.

> Just as the stream finds a bed that is lowly,
> So Jesus walks with the pure and the holy;
> Cast out thy pride, and in heartfelt contrition,
> Humble thyself to walk with God.
> — J. Oatman.

But there is something about deepest humility which makes men bold. For utter obedience is self-forgetful obedience. No longer do we hesitate and shuffle and apologize. . . . But self-renunciation means God-possession, the being possessed by God. Out of utter humility and self-forgetfulness comes the thunder of the prophets: "Thus saith the Lord." — Thomas Kelly in *A Testament of Devotion*.

The School of Humility

And what doth the LORD require of thee, but to do justly, and to love mercy, and to walk humbly with thy God? (Mic. 6:8).

GERHARD Tersteegen, contemporary with Zinzendorf, Wesley, and Whitefield, was a German mystic and evangelist. Through much solitude in God's presence he was highly favored with many secrets of the Lord. Without effort of his own he was sought out in his seclusion by the hungry in the land who hung on his words, sang his hymns, and walked in the Lord's way. The following excerpts from his letters and diaries show one of the secrets he learned:

"The poorer, the more humble and destitute we are, the more unreservedly, freely, and purely can we unite ourselves with God and His children, and the more capable are we of the participation of the divine favor. It was once whispered in my heart, 'Come like a naked infant, and then shall My bosom receive thee.' Self-love makes us afraid of mortification and privation, and represents them to us in a melancholy light. But the reverse is the truth, for as soon as they are cheerfully submitted to, they are found to be pleasing and salutary. But as long as we refuse them admittance, they produce sorrow of heart and countenance, and are often the occasion of many tedious sufferings. 'Christ humbled himself' (Phil. 2). We cannot humble ourselves, but must let ourselves be humbled. Christ humbles us by His guidance of us, and by His Spirit, and thus He makes us acceptable to God, in and through Him. This ought to be a great consolation, even for the most miserable, because they need only to approach as such, in order to receive from God every needful grace and virtue.

"O God! Thou seest that I know myself to be but a poor, weak, and helpless infant. Enable me ever to rejoice, when others know me to be so, and make no account of me. But although I be such an one as Thine eye seeth me to be, Thou hast nevertheless given me to love Thee, although much less than I ought, and infinitely less than Thou deservest, but I have this confidence, that in Thy light I have become acquainted with Thee and Thy truth, and behold and place in Thee alone, all my felicity.

"How wonderful, how incomprehensible are the ways of God! How contrary to our expectations! No sooner do we think of fetching breath a little, than we are again chased out. We never cease losing, till we become so poor that we have nothing more to lose, and so ashamed that we dare no longer look about us. Let us only persevere in God's name! May He alone be exalted, glorified, and well-pleased, that by thoroughly forsaking ourselves, we may enter into His felicity, His rest, and His joy! We must at length be brought to look on, as innocently as an infant in the cradle. It becomes us cheerfully to consent, deeply to adore, and cordially to say, 'The Lord is good and gracious: all His ways are mercy and truth,' without examining on what the expression is founded. Even in the full consciousness of our utter poverty and wretchedness, we cannot help wishing that every soul were equally poor. O how seldom do we meet with those who are entirely God's, and yet how happy are such characters! The Lord willingly becomes their portion, their treasure, their all.

"Expect nothing from yourself, but everything from the goodness of God, which is inwardly so near you."

> Where is the school for each and all,
> Where men become as children small,
> And little ones are great?
> Where love is all the task and rule;
> The fee our all and all at school,
> Small, poor, of low estate?
> Where to unlearn all things I learn,
> From self and from all others turn,
> One Master hear and see?
> I learn and do one thing alone,
> And wholly give myself to One
> Who gives Himself to me.
>
> —Tersteegen.

Poverty of Spirit

The LORD taketh pleasure in his people: he will beautify the meek with salvation (Psa. 149:4).

JOHN Fletcher, the Vicar of Madeley, although belonging to the Church of England, found his heart knit to the Methodists to whom he owed the light that brought him salvation. John Wesley admired this humble man who had chosen a lowly church position in an obscure mining village in the North of England and esteemed him as one of the godliest men of his wide acquaintance. He endeavored to prevail upon him to succeed him as the Chief Shepherd of the Methodist flock. John Fletcher was reluctant to give his assent, and his death at fifty-three took the matter out of man's hands.

His own talents were considerable as may be seen when reading his works, *Checks to Antinomianism*. His ancestral home was a prestigious one overlooking Lake Constance in the Swiss Alps. Coming from ancestors who had been in the military, it was thought that he would follow the family tradition, but a striking providence helped decide otherwise. As a result, the religious world has been enriched by his saintly life and the productions of his pen.

John Fletcher did not entertain views of his own saintliness which others accorded to him. He would lie prostrate on the floor whole nights, pleading with God to subdue the strong man and keep him meek and lowly. In a letter to Charles Wesley he bewails his lack: "A few days ago, the Lord gave me two or three lessons on the subject of poverty of spirit, but alas! how have I forgotten them! I saw, I felt, that I was entirely void of wisdom and virtue. I was ashamed of myself, and I could say with a degree of feeling, which I cannot describe, 'I do nothing, have nothing, am nothing; I crawl in the dust.' I could then say, what Gregory Lopez was enabled to say at all times, 'There is no man, of whom I have not a better opinion, than of myself.' I could have placed myself under the feet of the most atrocious sinner, and have acknowledged him for a saint in comparison of myself.

"If ever I am humble and patient, if ever I enjoy solid peace of mind, it must be in this very spirit. Ah! why do I not actually find these virtues: because I am filled with self-sufficiency, and am possessed by that self-esteem, which blinds me, and hinders me from doing justice to my own demerits. Oh! pray that the spirit of Jesus may remove these scales from my eyes forever, and compel me to retire into my own nothingness."

After his death, his beloved wife, Mary, discovered a medal which had been awarded him and of which he had never spoken. The King of England was so impressed with one of his pamphlets, that he offered him preferment in the Church of England. "I want nothing but more grace," was Fletcher's characteristic reply.

Henry Venn relates how, in his associations with Mr. Fletcher, he noted how unfeigned was his humility and how spontaneous his hatred of personal gratification. He says: "When I thanked him for two sermons he had one day preached to my people at Huddersfield, he answered as no man ever did to me. With eyes and hands uplifted, he exclaimed, 'Pardon, pardon, pardon, O my God.' The words went to my very soul. Great grace was upon this blessed servant of Christ."

Lord, Thou dost the grace impart!
Poor in spirit, meek in heart,
I shall as my Master be
Rooted in humility.

Now, dear Lord, that Thee I know,
Nothing will I seek below,
Aim at nothing great or high,
Lowly both in heart and eye.
— Unknown.

154

Continuing Dependence

As the branch cannot bear fruit of itself, except it abide in the vine; no more can ye, except ye abide in me (John 15:4).

GEORGE Bowen was a very talented man who went to India as a missionary and was resident there for many years, refusing to take even one furlough. He defied the usual customs of former missionaries, living more simply and depending upon God for His leading and finance. He learned many secrets from the Lord. We share one of them with you:

"Christians often err in estimating fruit. Success is often latent, coming slowly to light, and that which is more rapid and conspicuous may turn out at last to have been the opposite of success. He that is sincerely bent on bringing forth much fruit to Christ will rest with satisfaction in this conception alone, mainly, that the favor of God is fruit. Am I doing that which has the approbation of the almighty Disposer of all? If I am, then I am bringing forth the best possible fruit. It will appear in His own good time, though it should be a thousand years hence.

"One man insists on seeing his fruit, and God gives way to him and lets him have what he seeks; he sees his work prospering in his hands, but, unhappily, it does not endure; there is in the end the bitterness of disappointment. Another asks but one thing—that he may please to the uttermost Him Who has called him to be His servant. He is willing to wait in apparent sterility until God shall give the increase. He knows that God is the Author of all true fruit and has the absolute control of all resources, and can accomplish by the wave of His hand the renovation of the world. Accordingly he puts his seed into the hand of God, sure that, in the best of times, he will see the best of harvests. Let us abide in Christ, bury ourselves in Him, be found in Him. 'Except a corn of wheat fall into the ground

155

and die, it abideth alone; but if it die, it bringeth forth much fruit.'

"'Without me (or apart from me) ye can do nothing' — nothing in the way of bringing forth fruit to Christ. What we do without a reference to Christ, without a conscious dependence upon Him, without a desire to please Him, we do without His approbation. It is not His will that we should do anything without Him, and, therefore, whatsoever we do without Him, we do against His will. In such a matter as finding the colt for Christ to sit upon, even, it was needful that the disciples should abide in Christ."

Bishop Lightfoot makes a similar observation: "In our eagerness for immediate visible results, it is well to remember that the price of haste is brief duration; that anything which ripens before its time withers before its time, and that in all the works of God there is a conspicuous absence of all hurry. . . . The word indeed ran very swiftly, but it was the word of Him Whose earthly life had been spent in an obscure village of Galilee, never hurrying, never precipitating, biding His time, waiting patiently till His hour was come. How true a figure of the Church's progress was the leaven hid in the measures of meal! What a weary period it must have seemed to the faithful of the early days, when the early Church worked her way in the literal sense of the word, underground, under camp and palace, under Senate and Forum, as unknown and yet well-known, as dying and behold it lived."

From one of the best commentators, Frederick Godet, we have this comment: "Man was not so created as to be able to reach his ideal by drawing the required strength from his own resources. He can only attain to that by the aid of continual communications from God. Now, as soon as he gives way to the sway of an evil power, these communications are interrupted; he does not any longer ask for, or receive them. Retrogression then takes the place of progress. Like a plant torn from its natural soil, man vegetates and perishes, instead of growing and bearing fruit."

Limited — Unlimited

The lofty looks of man shall be humbled, and the haughtiness of men shall be bowed down, and the LORD alone shall be exalted in that day. For the day of the LORD of hosts shall be upon every one that is proud and lofty, and upon every one that is lifted up; and he shall be brought low (Isa. 2: 11, 12).

THERE are two characteristic marks which govern in our human nature capacity, and in the structural law of being:

1. We are limited.

2. We are utterly dependent upon God. We have no independence outside of Him. He never gives His power (in the Greek — "exhousia" and "dunamis") to anyone. He lent His power to Adam.

In creation, God made man limited and dependent — two chief characteristics of the human. Man *is dependent upon God,* for there is no life in himself; he is a created being, and *he is limited* to moving within the sphere of the natural bounds. Of the human nature, God said, "I will make it dependent and limited. I will make him dependent so that man cannot of himself do anything, but, as I give him life and strength, and My will is revealed, he will take his will and attach it to Mine, and We will work together."

Man didn't originate anything. God originated all the planning; Adam was to execute it as limited and dependent man.

Jesus was a completely consecrated instrument in the hands of God for the display of God's grace and power. "He that hath seen Me hath seen the Father. I don't originate anything. The Words that I speak (the message), are God's; the power that I have is God's. I am the Last Adam. I am functioning, but there is no independence in Me, nor in any of the Trinity."

Concerning the Spirit, He says, "When He, the Spirit, is come, He will take of the things that I have given, and show them unto you." He will not speak *from* Himself—not: "He will not speak *of* Himself." ("Of" is a poor preposition.) He speaks *of* Himself in His ministry hundreds of times, but He never speaks *from* Himself as an authority. "He will take the things that I have given, and speak them unto you." Why? To keep that strange dramatic unity in the whole scheme: the Father, the Son, the Holy Spirit.

I like His yieldedness and His absolute surrender. It astounds me! The more I see Him, the more I marvel at this Christ—the most tremendous character that ever walked the earth; the most sublime personality that ever touched the earth! (John 14:1-11). . . .

We are not on a picnic; we are in a warfare. We are engaged in a battle. We are in a tremendous process of being extricated and conformed. God is dealing with us drastically; sometimes most ferociously, and sometimes very tenderly. He wants to extricate us—to get us on the grounds where we belong, with our vision where it should be, and to teach us how to walk with Him in the Spirit.

The discipline I may call forth from God takes a life-time. It is good we don't see very much before. He can't trust us with it. If I had known what I had to go through the last twenty-five years, I don't know if I would have had the courage to face it. —John Wright Follette.

> I am a flame born of celestial fire;
> I bear a name, Insatiable Desire.
>
> I wear in heart an image all divine,
> Past human art, not traced by mortal line.
>
> I hear God call to taste His heavenly power:
> I give my all to burn life's single hour.
>
> So let me burn through fetters that would bind;
> Thus will I learn and freedom will I find.
>
> I shall return to Love's eternal fire,
> There shall I burn—a satisfied desire.
> —John Wright Follette.

The Child Mood

Suffer little children, and forbid them not, to come unto me: for of such is the kingdom of heaven (Matt 19:14).

WE often think and speak and hear about being saved up into the higher degrees of Christ, and this is proper; but let us remember that it is equally important to be saved down, down to things small and lowly.

Many years since, God lifted upon me His reconciled countenance and gave me a place in His kingdom, but that other change, spoken of by Christ, viz., to become a little child, I am entering into more fully of late than ever before. God is carrying me down, down into the child mood. How I frequently realize this in prayer! I seem to go back to my blessed childhood. There is the same feeling of utter dependence, and yet of perfect security; the same forgetfulness of everything sinful and unholy, so that I come to be only conscious of things that are pure. I seem to know how Jesus took the little children into His arms and blessed them. I remember how, when I was a child, I read that passage over and over again, and wished that I could have been one of that company of children, and that Jesus had taken me into His arms and blessed me. But since then, I have many times known that same Jesus still takes the little children in His arms and blesses them.

Spiritual childhood is better than natural childhood, for it combines all that is good in a child's heart with what is valuable in that same heart when matured. The trust may be stronger and more perfect, and purity purer, something much more than the innocence of ignorance. — Alfred Cookman.

Childhood often holds a truth with its feeble finger, which the grasp of manhood cannot retain, which it is the pride of utmost age to recover. — John Ruskin.

The nature of a little child,
I simply could not see
How such a nature ever could
Become a part of me.

The pride of years would never let
My Savior on the Throne,
But crowned me King and kept me where
I reigned, just I alone

This pride, oh, what a horrid thing,
Kept me from bending low,
So through the kingdom's door, you see,
I simply could not go. . . .

Then, oh the wonder of that day,
I saw what I should do;
I said, "Lord Jesus, I step down
And give the throne to You."

And so when I by faith obeyed,
A miracle of grace
Within this haughty heart of mine,
That moment did take place. . . .

Now would I, dare I, could I try
Once more the Kingdom's door?
I longed to, yet it looked so low,
So near unto the floor.

But beckoned by the pierced Hand
Which had removed my sin,
Upon my knees, now weak and small,
A child, I entered in. . . .

And so, diminished as I am,
Stripped of all else but grace,
I live, a trusting little child.
And look upon His face. . . .

—Trudy Tait.

Profound or Childlike?

Who is the greatest in the kingdom of heaven? And Jesus called a little child unto him . . . and said . . . Except ye be converted, and become as little children, ye shall not enter into the kingdom of heaven (Matt. 18:1-3).

WE are a generation of tired, fussy little Christians, experts but not examples. We know too much. We have heard all the preachers and read all the books. It is hard these days to be converted and become like little children. We want to be thought philosophers and scholars and brilliant—but childlike? Never! Somebody would think we were dumb, so we miss the secrets God has hidden from the wise and prudent and revealed unto babes. Not many wise, mighty, noble have been called, but we go on trying to be wise, mighty, and noble.

It is possible, of course, for a rich man to get into the kingdom, and for a learned man to become like a child, but not many of them do it. How often, even among the saints, does some simple soul learn the deeper things of God and press through to Heaven's best while theologians utterly miss them! We know too much. —Vance Havner.

As Vinet says, the passage from knowledge to possession, from belief to life, our Lord has strikingly represented by the figure, so singular at first sight, of a return from mature age to childhood. "Except ye be converted, and become as little children, ye cannot enter the kingdom of heaven." And the beautiful profound truth hidden under this paradox is, that not only are the spirit of childhood and the spirit of manhood not inconsistent with each other, but their union is essential to the highest spiritual culture. The human soul never is so great as when it humbles itself in childlike meekness to be a learner at the feet of divine wisdom.

—Hugh Macmillan.

161

That very pertinent writer, Oswald Chambers, has said: "Beware of posing as a profound person; God became a Baby."

The disciples measured themselves by their manliness; Jesus taught them to measure themselves by their childlikeness. —Joseph Parker.

Let us notice that Jesus specifically mentions *little children,* and not just *children.* The Savior knew that the *little* child is in the best possible position for the acceptance of others exactly as they are, without a display on his part of superiority, pride, embarrassment, or resentment toward them, because the *little* child has learned to accept himself on precisely those terms. Being little, he has had to modify the goals, drives, and capacities of his larger fellows, and by being himself is actually living a fuller form of life within his self-imposed limits than is often the case with others.
—Professor R. K. Harrison.

> Since, Lord, to Thee,
> A narrow way and little gate
> Is all the passage, on my infancy
> Thou didst lay hold, and antedate
> My faith in me.
>
> O let me still
> Write Thee, great God, and me, a child:
> Let me be soft and supple to Thy will,
> Small to myself, to others mild,
> Behither ill.   (except in anything evil.)
> —George Herbert.

The Beautiful Presence hides itself more in babes than in men. It is marvelous in our eyes, that where there is neither physical might nor rational might, *there* the God of all might should be so much the more. But so it is. "Out of the mouth of babes and sucklings hast thou ordained strength."
—John Pulsford in *Quiet Thoughts.*

Acquire Meekness

Now the man Moses was very meek, above all the men which were upon the face of the earth (Num. 12:3)
Seek meekness: it may be ye shall be hid in the day of the LORD'S anger (Zeph. 2:3).

BY all accounts, Moses did not begin by being a meek man. The truth is, no truly meek man ever does so begin. It is not true meekness if it is found in any man at the beginning of his life. It may be sloth, it may be softness, it may be easiness, it may be indifference, it may be policy and calculation, it may be insensibility of heart, it may be sluggishness of blood, but true meekness it is not. True meekness it is not until it has been planted, and watered, and pruned, and purified, and beaten upon by every wind of God, and cut to pieces by every knife of God, and all the time engrafted and seated deep in the meekness and in the gentleness and in the humility of the Spirit of God and the Son of God.

It would be far nearer the truth to say that Moses, to begin with, was the hastiest and the hottest and the least meek and the least long-suffering of men. It was but a word and a blow with young Moses. . . . No, the meekness of Moses was not a case of complexion, nor a matter of temperament any more than it was the grace of a new beginner in godliness and virtue. Moses would by that time be well on to three-score and ten of our years, as we count our years, before it was written of him what stands written of him in our noble text. — Alexander Whyte in *Bible Characters*.

Never allow yourself to answer again when you are blamed. Never defend yourself. Let them reprehend you, in private or in public, as much as they please. Let the righteous smite you, it shall be a kindness; and let him reprove you, it shall be an excellent oil which shall not break your head.

"It is a mark of the deepest and truest humility," says a great saint, "to see ourselves condemned without cause and to be silent under it. To be silent under insult and wrong is a very noble imitation of our Lord. O my Lord, when I remember in how many ways Thou didst suffer, Who in no way deserved it, I know not where my senses are when I am in such haste to defend and excuse myself.

"Is it possible I should desire anyone to speak any good of me or to think it, when so many ill things were thought and spoken of Thee! What about being blamed by all men, if only we stand at last blameless before Thee!"

— Alexander Whyte.

Henry Bett in a periodical relates how Dr. Whyte fully acted upon his advice to others when he himself was reprehended. "Some revivalists of the more ignorant and bigoted type were holding meetings in Edinburgh. Someone who had attended some of these gatherings told Dr. Whyte that one of the missioners had said that Dr. J. Hood Wilson, was 'not a converted man.'

"Dr. Whyte was most indignant, 'The scoundrels!' he said, 'to say that of a man like Dr. Hood Wilson!' Then the informant went on. 'And they said that you were not a converted man either.' Dr. Whyte was silent for a moment. Then he said, 'Leave me, my friend: I must look into my heart.' That is a perfect illustration of the spirit of genuine humility. He was angry, and rightly angry, that anything so untrue and unkind should be said of another man, but when it was said of himself he did not resent it, but only searched his heart to find whether there was any truth in the charge.

"No wonder that Dr. James Denny paid Dr. Whyte the tribute that he did in one of his letters, where he said that Dr. Smellie was the humblest man he knew, 'except Dr. Whyte.' That afterthought is a superb testimony — Dr. Whyte did not come into the comparison at all; he stood apart. . . ."

The True Nobility

Take my yoke upon you, and learn of me; for I am meek and lowly in heart: and ye shall find rest unto your souls (Matt. 11:29).

I AM sure there are many Christians who will confess that their experience has been very much like my own in this, that we had long known the Lord without realizing that meekness and lowliness of heart are to be the distinguishing feature of the disciple as they were of the Master. And further that this humility is not a thing that will come of itself, but that it must be made the object of special desire and prayer and faith and practice.

The call to humility has been too little regarded in the Church, because its true nature and importance has been too little apprehended. It is not a something which we bring to God, or He bestows; it is simply the sense of entire nothingness, which comes when we see how truly God is all, and in which we make way for God to be all. When the creature realizes that this is the true nobility and consents to be, with his will, his mind, and his affections, the form, the vessel in which the life and glory of God are to work and manifest themselves, he sees that humility is simply acknowledging the truth of his position as creature, and yielding to God His place.

In the life of earnest Christians, of those who pursue and profess holiness, humility ought to be the chief mark of their uprightness. It is often said that it is not so. May not one reason be that in the teaching and example of the Church, it has never had that place of supreme importance which belongs to it? And that this, again, is owing to the neglect of this truth, that strong as sin is as a motive to humility, there is one of still wider and mightier influence, that which makes the angels, that which made Jesus, that which makes the holiest of saints in Heaven, so humble—that the first and chief mark of the relation of the creature, the secret of his blessedness, is the humility and nothingness which leaves God free to be all? —Andrew Murray.

The man with earthly wisdom high uplifted
 Is in God's sight a fool;
But he in heavenly truth most deeply gifted,
 Sits lowest in Christ's school.

The lowly spirit God hath consecrated
 As His abiding rest;
And angels by some Patriarch's tent have waited,
 When Kings had no such guests.

The dew that never wets a flinty mountain,
 Falls in the valleys free;
Bright verdure fringes the small desert-fountain,
 But barren sand the sea.

The censer swung by the proud hand of merit,
 Fumes with a fire abhorr'd;
But faith's two mites, dropp'd covertly, inherit
 A blessing from the Lord.

         — Unknown.

It takes us all our days to learn these two things — to be meek and to be lowly. — Unknown.

Circumcision was a sign that marked out the Jew from the rest of mankind. What is the corresponding mark of our Christian life before men? Is it charity? Wisdom? Sincerity? Zeal? Other men have these. None of them is peculiar to the people of God, but there is one that is. It is a seemly absence of self-confidence! What distinguishes God's own is that their confidence in the flesh is destroyed and they are cast back upon Him. I have known Christians who are so sure they know the will of God that they will not for one moment consider they may be mistaken. I tell you they still lack the supreme sign of the spiritual "circumcision," namely, no confidence in the flesh. The spiritual man walks humbly, always aware he may be wrong. He assents gladly to the apocryphal beatitude: Happy are they who realize they may be mistaken! — Watchman Nee in *A Table in the Wilderness.*

The God-Tamed Ones

Blessed are the meek: for they shall inherit the earth (Matt. 5:5).

J. B. PHILLIPS translates the above verse as, "Happy are they who claim nothing, for the whole earth belongs to them." The Greek word for meekness is *praotes* which does not suggest weakness or mildness but great power under control.

I think the best example I have seen of this was when watching the changing of the guards in front of Buckingham Palace in London. The Horse Guard is made up of magnificently trained horses, whose quivering nostrils and taut muscles betoken control of superabundant strength and energy. Often, the feet are moving as if marking time. Now and then, the horse moves a bit forward, but the rider pulls him in with the rein; he may even turn a complete circle only to be brought back to his former position. He is always raring to go, but must wait for his master's command.

Perhaps you have seen a similar display of meekness when observing a mounted policeman, thronged on every side by excited crowds. His magnificent horse, displaying such tremendous potential for movement, is reined to stand there, while the crowds surge about him.

The Bible, of course, has much to tell us about true meekness. Moses was the greatest example of a meek man. Raring to free his fellowmen, he gets out of rein and does damage. But he learns his lesson and is meek enough to wait God's perfect timing on the backside of the desert, tending not even his own sheep but those of his father-in-law.

Most of our mistakes stem from our getting out of rein and failing to move in time with God's eternal purposes. James Caughey observed this with regard to the marriages of some of his ministerial friends. It was not that they had made a mistake in marrying the woman of their choice, but in moving out of God's time.

Many missionaries, impatient because of God's seeming slowness, have also moved out of time with the Divine plan. Arriving on the mission-field ahead of His timing, they have thus missed learning the valuable lessons which God saw would have prepared them for a field of service which would be bristling with difficulties. Reproofs, too, which were necessary in God's own time, have often been given in man's own time and have therefore proved ineffectual. Even purchasing a car or a house, or the performing of our acts of benevolence—all must be done in meekness by waiting for the Lord's proper time. "Waiting" is a word used often in the Bible because it is so vital that we learn to wait.

—Lillian Harvey.

Meekness is a state of flexibility in the hand of God and a condition of inflexibility to evil. It is a domestic word used of a disciplined animal. Meekness is self-control and like the mighty engine can polish a needle or cut a bar of iron. It is man's spirit under the control of God's Spirit.

Blessed are the tamed, the balanced, the disciplined, the God-controlled, the teachable, the pilgrims of the middle road of God, the giants who by the Spirit resist every evil impulse and set in motion and harness every good inclination to the glory of God. For they shall rule as kings and reign as lords in the regeneration of all things. —Oswald Chambers.

The God-moulded ones—the Hebrew word.
The God-tamed ones—the Greek word.
The God-trained ones—the French word.
The God-tempered ones—the German word.
—Edward Angell.

The timber of the elder tree is the softest and can without difficulty be split, cut, and wrought, and yet experience proves that it does not rot in water. The greater part of Venice stands upon piles of elder which, sunk in the sea, form the foundation of massive buildings. The pillars of meekness will defy all storms, tests, persecutions and floods of contradiction. —Unknown.

Self-Forgetting Service

Above it stood the seraphims: each one had six wings; with twain he covered his face, and with twain he covered his feet (Isa. 6:2).

THOSE angelic beings in heavenly places show, by their very posture, with what humble adoration they worship. Phillips Brooks gives some thought-provoking comments on this: "A quality of consecrated power is indicated by the wings with which, in the vision of the seraphim, each seraph covered his feet, or, indeed, his whole person.

"This quality of self-effacement or self-forgetfulness enters into all good work, and most of all, into the best. A great work apparently does itself. Some day the humble doer awakens and, behold, the work is done, and he is famous, and he himself is astonished. He only knew that there was a great wrong to resist, and he had no choice but to be at it. So men have conducted themselves in battle; the fortress must be taken and the sally made, and it was done without thought of glory.

"The loss of this quality of self-forgetfulness spoils a good work. The governor of a state is going on nobly with measures of public beneficence; he holds the people's confidence until some day they perceive he is calculating the value of his own policy for his own political ends. A friend comes to advise with me. I take his admonition as precious balm, his commendations as proof of his affection until he ruins all that he has said with one lurid flash of self-consciousness. He has shown that he is thinking chiefly of his own wisdom and superiority.

"Efface yourself if you would have your work stand. Do it, as it only can be done, by standing in the presence of God. Yet this self-effacement is also represented in the vision of wings. Self must be lost behind the activity of self. There is no other way to become unconscious but to lose one's self in his work. It is not because men make so much of their work, but because they make so little of it that they cannot forget themselves in it.

"'Yonder is myself without the inconvenience of myself,' said Lacordaire, when his brother monk was elevated over his head."

Hide Thou Thy servant, Lord, behind Thy cross
    That but Thyself, Thy beauty, may appear—
    Thy touching truth that pricks the heart to hear;
Poor human words could bring to Thee but loss.
Speak Thou the veil from Heaven to earth across;
    Thy precepts speak into each listening ear;
    Let doubt give way, defiance drop a tear;
Lord, hide Thy servant well behind Thy cross!

Then shall Thy testimonies pure unfold;
    Then shall be seen Heaven's altar-fire aglow;
With Spirit-power shall be Thy Words and bold;
    Then freely shall Thy loving-kindness flow,
Thy tender mercies, golden, pure of dross,
If Thou but hide Thy messenger behind Thy cross!
                            —Jean Leathers Phillips.

One day a friend of mine, when passing down a Glasgow street, saw a crowd at a shop door, and had the curiosity to look in. There he saw an auctioneer holding up a grand picture so that all could see it. When he got it into position, he remained behind it and said to the crowd, "Now, look at this part of the picture . . . and now at this other part," and so on, describing each detail of it. Said my friend, "The whole time I was there, I never saw the speaker, but only the picture he was showing." That is the way to work for Christ. —Andrew Bonar.

It is when we forget ourselves that we do things that are remembered. —Eugene P. Bertin.

Self-forgetting work is heavenly work. —Unknown.

He who is seeking recognition is as a rule soon recognized—and little appreciated. —T. Rotide.

Secret Service

When thou doest alms, let not thy left hand know what thy right hand doeth: That thine alms may be in secret (Matt. 6:3,4).
Enter into thy closet, and when thou hast shut thy door, pray to thy Father which is in secret (Matt. 6: 6).
Anoint thine head, and wash thy face; That thou appear not unto men to fast, but unto thy Father which is in secret (Matt. 6: 17,18).

IF we were to put our Christian service under the searchlight of the Holy Spirit, we would be surprised to find how much of it had its driving force in a desire to be highly esteemed among men. How many church activities are successful because they have the element of competition in them! Without that impetus, the drive for new members or for a more pretentious building would lag. God is looking for purity of motives in our service. He penalized the double-minded, the one who served two masters—Christ and self.

All service rendered reaps a reward. If it is done with an eye to pleasing people, then verily "they have their reward." "No reward" from the Father is to be expected if we have the glory of man in view. God rewards secret service. Unlike the kingdom of this world where there is much of showmanship and display before men, God's kingdom is one where service is done only for the Father.

When David Livingstone was asked by his home committee to send records of his converts, he disdained such a request. He felt that if he reported fifty souls saved when his Father only recorded one, what would be the worth of such statistics. In the twentieth century, there is the same demand for statistics. I can remember a tired and weary minister who had to hasten from his morning service in order to send records of attendance and offerings to the headquarters of his denomination. Competition with another church was being used to motivate him.

The service which is secret is misunderstood because it has no present, outward glory. This tests the faith of the doer. Such secret service requires three things: faith in an invisible Person, pure motivation or a single eye, and a reward that is future instead of *now*.

The praise which comes from man is very short-lived: the reward for secret service is of an everlasting quality. How can our faith be tested if man who can be seen is more prominent in our vision than the invisible God? Our faith is sorely tried when we see fellow Christians succeeding by methods approved by the religious world. Their statistics are published. Their church building is magnificent. Our associates look on, unaware of our secret efforts and ask, "What is he doing?" Many of us who have sought to live out the principles of the "Sermon on the Mount" know how frequently these trials to our faith arise. But Peter says, "The trial of your faith, being much more precious than of gold that perisheth, though it be tried with fire, might be found unto praise and honor and glory at the appearing of Jesus Christ."

Christ set us an example in this secret service. After His visit to Jerusalem at the age of twelve, He spent eighteen years in obscurity and only three short years in active ministry. His own brethren challenged this secret type of service; when they were ready to go up to the feast at Jerusalem and He was not going with them, they expostulated, "There is no man that doeth any thing in secret, and he himself seeketh to be known openly. If thou do these things, shew thyself to the world." His brethren did not believe in Him because His methods were so other-worldly. Jesus' answer showed them that He had a constant communion with the Father, from Whom He received not only His directions as to His speaking, His works, His judgments, but even with regard to the timing of His comings and goings. "Your time is always," Jesus said to His brothers; "My time is not yet come."

The cross will be present in such a secret service. Are we ready for it? — Lillian Harvey.

Unmindful of Who Gets the Credit

That both he that soweth and he that reapeth may rejoice together. And herein is that saying true, One soweth, and another reapeth (John 4:36,37).

SOMEONE has well said that there is plenty of work to do in the world if you don't care who gets the credit. Jesus gave His heavenly Father the credit for His converts. In His last prayer in the seventeenth chapter of John, Christ mentions seven times, "Those thou hast given me."

Robert Murray McCheyne was a godly young minister who had organized over thirty prayer-meetings in his large parish in Perth in the north of Scotland. Aware of the danger of taking the credit, he said: "It is our truest happiness to live entirely for the glory of Christ—to separate between 'I' and 'the glory of Christ.' We are always saying, 'What have I done? Was it my preaching, my sermon, my influence?' Whereas we should be asking, 'What hath God wrought?'"

He continued to urge his people: "I charge you, be clothed with humility, or you will be a wandering star for which is reserved the blackness of darkness forever. Let Christ increase; let man decrease. This is my constant prayer for myself and you."

When laid aside by sickness, McCheyne was sorely tested and wrote: "Paul asked, 'What wilt thou have me to do?' And it was answered, 'I will show him what great things he must suffer for my name's sake.' Thus it may be with me. I have been too anxious to do great things. The lust of praise has ever been my besetting sin, and what more befitting school could be found for me than that of suffering alone, away from the eye and ear of man."

He was being prepared for what was to follow, when, because of ill health, he was sent by the synod of the Church of Scotland with a party of other ministers to search out the condition of Jews abroad. "I sometimes think," he said, "that a great blessing may come to my people in my absence. Often God does not bless us when we are in the midst of our labors, lest we shall say, 'My hand and my eloquence have done it.' He removes us into silence, and then pours down a blessing so that there is no room to receive it, so that all that see it cry out, 'It is the Lord.'"

Andrew Bonar, his biographer, said: "Mr. McCheyne very earnestly sought from the Lord one to supply his pulpit during his absence. The Lord abundantly granted his desire by sending Mr. William C. Burns, son of the minister of Kilsyth. In a letter to him, the following remarkable words occur: 'You are given in answer to prayer, and these gifts are, I believe, always without exception, blessed. I hope you may be a thousand times more blessed among them than ever I was. Perhaps there are many souls that would never have been saved under my ministry who may be touched under yours: and God has taken this method of bringing you into my place. His name is Wonderful.'"

And God did pour out revival blessing under William Burns' ministry; the former sower had done his work well, and now the reaper came to harvest the fruit. William Burns, however, though in this instance so mightily blessed as a reaper, later went to China where he sowed the seed for years but saw not the fruit.

> In the deed that no man knoweth,
> Where no praiseful trumpet bloweth,
> Where he may not reap who soweth,
> There, Lord, let my heart serve Thee.
> —Unknown.

The best part of Christian work is that part which only God sees. —Unknown.

I have planted, Apollos watered; but God gave the increase. So then neither is he that planteth any thing, neither he that watereth: but God that giveth the increase (1Cor. 3:6,7).

The Collapse of Self-Confidence

But thou, O man of God, flee these things; and follow after . . . meekness
(1 Tim. 6: 11).

A STRIKING characteristic of Dr. Maclaren was his
profound humility," said his biographer, J. Flew. "Someone has spoken of his 'monstrous shyness.' I dislike the expression. It is true that he was naturally shy, so much so that
he shrank from meeting men of outstanding position and influence. . . .

"He never through his long life ceased to feel 'the aw-
fully conspicuous position of a pulpit;' and he felt it was only
the necessity of the preacher's being distinctly seen and heard
that justified it. But 'shyness' is not the word that covers that
sensitiveness to prominence and very much else that is akin
to it. Neither is it enough to say that he was entirely free from
anything approaching to egotism, so that it was impossible
for him to speak of his own doings. Back of all these things,
and in some sense the cause of them, there was in him, as I
have said, a genuine, deep-rooted humility. He was God's
messenger; his mission was to set forth 'Christ and Him crucified,' and how could a man be aggressive and self-assertive
when he realized that?

"'To efface one's self,' he said, 'is one of a preacher's first
duties. The herald should be lost in his message.' And he
himself so far succeeded that one typical testimony to the effect of his preaching was borne by a farmer's wife, who said:
'I never heard anything like yon prayers and sermons; I can
hear him now; and the strange thing was, I never, at the time,
thought about its being Dr. Maclaren that we all knew and
liked. . . .'

"When a letter was read to him, speaking of him as a
guide and teacher whose name called forth feelings of gratitude and veneration wherever it was mentioned, in a pained
tone he said: 'Oh, stop! I cannot listen to words like these.

When I woke this morning and thought, I said to myself, "A sinner saved by grace, that is all."'"

In one of his sermons, "The Collapse of Self-Confidence," Maclaren says: "The world and the Church hold entirely antagonistic notions about the value of self-reliance. The world says that it is a condition of power. The Church says that it is the root of weakness. Self-confidence shuts a man out from the help of God and so shuts him out from the source of power. For if you will think for a moment, you will see that the faith which the New Testament, in conformity with all wise knowledge of one's own self, preaches as the one secret of power, has for its obverse—its other side—diffidence and self-distrust.

"No man trusts God as God ought to be trusted, who does not distrust himself as himself ought to be distrusted. To level a mountain is the only way to carry the water across where it stood. You can, by mechanism and locks, take a canal up to the top of a hill, but you cannot take a river up to the top. And the river of God's help flows through the valley and seeks the lowest levels.

"Faith and self-despair are the upper and the under sides of the same thing, like some cunningly-woven cloth, the one side bearing a different pattern from the other, and yet made of the same yarn, and the same threads passing from the upper to the under sides. So faith and self-distrust are but two names for one composite whole. . . .

"When thus, as Wesley has it in his great hymn, 'Confident in self-despair,' we cling to God, then we can say: 'When I am weak then am I strong.'"

> Live Christ—and though thy road may be
> The strait way of humility;
> He Who first trod that way of God
> Will clothe thee with His dignity.
> —John Oxenham.

No grace is so difficult for me as humility. I want a lowly mind. Pray for greater simplicity and particularly for singlness of aim and humility of mind—not ever to think of myself highly. —A. T. Pierson.

Not Ashamed to Bend

Put on therefore, as the elect of God, holy and beloved . . . humbleness of mind, meekness . . . Forbearing one another (Col. 3:12.13).

SOMEONE has said. "The test of our greatness is how we deal with littleness." And another has observed, "The time to test a true gentleman is to observe him when he is in contact with individuals of a race less fortunate than his own."

Stephen Merritt had provided a free meal for the down-and-outs who attended his mission in New York. He was about to leave, when, upon putting on his hat, scraps of bread and bacon rinds fell about his shoulders. This produced an outburst of laughter among the men as they watched the chagrin of their benefactor. Mounting a chair, Stephen Merritt roundly berated the men for their prank.

Suddenly, the Holy Spirit spoke to the irate minister, bringing to remembrance what Christ had said through His inspired words: "Love suffereth long and is kind . . . is not easily provoked . . . beareth all things." He had been a man sensitive to the promptings of the Holy Spirit, and so he humbly took the rebuke and told the men that he had grieved his Lord. He invited them back to another free meal the next night, and the response of the men was greater than he could have thought. Forty had been effected by his humble apology and opened their hearts to the Savior.

Robert Louis Stevenson had spoken roughly to one of his servants at the dinner table, but was later pricked in his heart, realizing that he had taken advantage of his employee who dared not defend herself. He was determined to make an apology, but it took him four days before he could get the courage to thus humble himself.

Professor Stewart Blackie of Edinburgh University was one day lecturing, when a student rose with the book in his left hand. The young man had begun an explanation when the Professor roared at him, "Take your book in your right hand and be seated."

The student never answered a word, but merely held up his right hand which had been severed at the wrist. The Professor hesitated a moment, and then, his face bathed with tears, went to the student, saying, "I never knew about it. Will you forgive me?"

Years later, when this story was told at a Bible conference, a man with his right arm severed at the wrist, arose and came forward saying, "I am the man that Professor Blackie led to Christ. But he never would have done it if he had not put his arms around me and made the wrong right."

Even in the political world there have been instances of greatness of character when men were not ashamed to bend. A newspaper reporter had written a scathing editorial criticizing the President of the Senate, Manuel Quezon. At a party that night in which both the president and the reporter were present, the latter received a severe tongue-lashing from the hot-tempered president. The following morning, to his surprise, Manuel Quezon was awaiting him. "I came to apologize," he said. "I had no right to talk to you the way I did last night. I am sorry."

"Quezon won my heart," confessed the reporter, "and from that moment on he had my abiding admiration. He grew tall. He was not ashamed to bend."

I could not do without Thee!
    I cannot stand alone:
I have no strength or goodness,
    No wisdom of my own.
But Thou, beloved Savior,
    Art all in all to me;
And weakness will be power,
    If leaning hard on Thee.
        — Frances Ridley Havergal.

Made Wise by Reproof

Poverty and shame shall be to him that refuseth instruction: but he that regardeth reproof shall be honoured (Prov. 13: 18).

WHEN people detect in us what are actually imperfections and faults, it is clear that they do us no wrong, since it is not they who caused them; and it is clear, too, that they do us a service, inasmuch as they help us to free ourselves from an evil, namely, the ignorance of these defects. We should not be angry because they know them and despise us; for it is right that they should know us for what we are, and that they should despise us if we are despicable.

Such are the feelings which would rise in a heart filled with equity and justice. What then should we say of our own heart when we see in it a quite contrary frame of mind? For is it not a fact that we hate the truth and those who tell it us, that we love those who deceive themselves in our favor, and that we wish to be esteemed by them as other than we really are? —Pascal.

We would rather be ruined by praise, than humbled by reproof. —Unknown.

> If a foe hath kenn'd,
> Or worse than foe, an alienated friend,
> A rib of dry rot in thy ship's stout side,
> Think it God's message, and in humble pride
> With heart of oak replace it: thine the gains!
> Give him the rotten timber for his pains!
> —Coleridge.

He that wrestles with us, strengthens our nerves and sharpens our skill. Our antagonist is our helper. —Edmund Burke.

179

Samuel Bradburn was one of Wesley's most eloquent speakers, but he received advice worth remembering from Joseph Benson, the Methodist commentator. He was complaining that he had just preached what seemed to him a poor sermon.

"I felt confident," said Bradburn, "as I ascended the pulpit stairs that I should have a successful time, but I came down miserably disappointed."

Benson shrewdly replied, "If you had gone up as you came down you would have come down as you went up."

Whoever is wise is apt to suspect and be diffident of himself, and upon that account is willing to "hearken unto counsel," whereas the foolish man, being, in proportion to his folly, full of himself and swallowed up in conceit, will seldom take any counsel but his own — and for that very reason — because it is his own. — Unknown.

If any speak ill of thee, flee home to thy own conscience, and examine thy heart; if thou be guilty, it is a correction; if not guilty, it is fair instruction; make use of both; so shalt thou distil honey out of gall, and out of an open enemy create a secret friend. — Quarles.

To take advice is no easy matter, and this, too, is a part of courage. We are all like men walking along a path backwards. No one can see the way till he has passed it, but those who are further on than we can see the stones and ditches that we are coming to, and if we listen to their directions, we shall avoid many hard falls and ugly slips. — Anon.

O Lord, I know that the way of man is not in himself: it is not in man that walketh to direct his steps. O LORD, correct me (Jer. 10:23,24).

Acknowledge Your Faults

Confess your faults one to another, and pray one for another, that ye may be healed (James 5:16).

ONE of the tests of humility is whether we are willing to acknowledge our faults or not. Wesley, writing to the Methodist people, warned: "'Be therefore clothed with humility.' Let it not only fill but cover you all over. Let modesty and self-diffidence appear in all your words and actions. Let all you speak and do, show that you are little, and base, and mean, and vile in your own eyes.

"As one instance of this, be always ready to own any fault you have been in. If you have at any time thought, spoken, or acted wrong, be not backward to acknowledge it. Never dream that this will hurt the cause of God; no, it will further it. Be, therefore, open and frank when you are taxed with anything; let it appear just as it is, and you will thereby not hinder but adorn the Gospel. Why should you be more backward in acknowledging your failings than in confessing that you do not pretend to infallibility?

"St. Paul was perfect in the love which casts out fear, and therefore he boldly reproved the high-priest, but when he had reproved him more sharply than the fifth commandment allows, he directly confessed his mistake, and set his seal to the importance of the duty in which he had been inadvertently wanting. Then Paul said, 'I knew not, brethren, that he was the high-priest: for it is written, Thou shalt not speak evil of the ruler of thy people.'"

A now venerable bishop was a man of commanding abilities, and at an unusually early age was placed at the head of a college. This nourished the propensity to self-confidence and vanity, which became conspicuous even to the students. While he would have died the next hour at the stake rather than deny his Lord, he was far from having died to his self-trust so that the Christ-life might fill his career. His stature was as much larger than most of other men as were his mental abilities.

One day he visited one of his students who was raving in a delirium of fever. As the young man caught sight of the large figure of his instructor, he turned on him and said wildly, "Great big Mr. President! Great big Mr. President! You think yourself some great one. When you preach you are so big that you hide the Cross; all that we see is great big Mr. President!"

The Lord by these delirious ravings, brought him to see his self-conceit — that self, and not Christ, had been uppermost. He at once went out "weeping bitterly" to a lonely spot in the woods, and there on his face, he confessed it all to his merciful Savior, and there learned the lesson of resurrection life. Forty years of eminently successful labor for Christ had borne the impress of that sacred hour of self-renunciation and trust. I heard him in his old age, tell this incident, with tears in his eyes, to a company of many hundred ministerial brethren. — Unknown.

The only hope for unconscious pride is to become aware of it. Reproof will show a person the way if he will be humble enough to take it. "Pride ," says Ruskin, "is at the bottom of great mistakes. Nor does it require experience of life to prove the truth of the dictum. The worst of it, however, is that pride seems to blind its victims. They are unconscious of any responsibility for the wreckage around them. The callous self has the eyes of the heart fast closed to what is obvious to every onlooker. So, locked up in steel, the proud soul wounds and knows it not; alienates and wonders at the shrinking; instructing but uninstructed."

Ambition is a gilded misery, a secret poison, a hidden plague, the engineer of deceit, the mother of hypocrisy, the parent of envy, the original of vices, the moth of holiness, the blinder of hearts, turning medicines into maladies and remedies into diseases. — St. Bernard.

To Whom Should We Listen?

Is there not here a prophet of the LORD besides, that we might enquire of him? . . . There is yet one man . . . by whom we may enquire of the LORD (1 Kings 22:7,8).

A TRULY humble man will always be open to the advice of others, for he feels he can learn from the lowliest of instruments. There are false prophets and advisers, however, who capitalize on this humility; they give fateful counsel to young believers and thus set them off course. We must ever recognize the voice of our Christ in the voice of our counselor. "My sheep hear my voice, a stranger will they not follow."

The example is before us in the Old Testament of Jehoshaphat who went to help Ahab in battle. Four hundred prophets were called by Ahab but Jehoshaphat was not satisfied until a true prophet of the Lord was engaged who was in the minority and differed from that of the majority. Jehoshaphat, however, took the wrong counsel and needed reproving: "Shouldest thou help the ungodly, and love them that hate the LORD?" (2 Chron. 19:2).

The whole kingdom of Judah suffered as a result of Jehoshaphat's misconduct. Athaliah married Jehoshaphat's son and later, when she ascended the throne, she sought to kill every descendant of David. Only by the discreet wisdom of God's high priest was there any male descendant of David left to carry on the line which God had prophesied should prevail. By listening to wrong advice, Jehoshaphat, who otherwise was a noble and good king, wreaked ruin upon the kingdom of Judah. — Lillian Harvey.

A. W. Tozer has a remarkable article in his book, *The Root of the Righteous,* in which he gives timely advice against listening without discrimination:

"In any group of ten persons at least nine are sure to believe that they are qualified to offer advice to others. And in no other field of human interest are people as ready to offer advice as in the field of religion and morals. Yet it is precisely in this field that the average person is least qualified to speak wisely and is capable of the most harm when he does speak. For this reason we should select our counselors carefully. And selection inevitably carries with it the idea of rejection.

"No man has any right to offer advice who has not first heard God speak. No man has any right to counsel others who is not ready to hear and follow the counsel of the Lord. True moral wisdom must always be an echo of God's voice. The only safe light for our path is the light which is reflected from Christ, the Light of the world.

"It is especially important that young people learn whose counsel to trust. Having been in the world for such a short time they have not had much experience and must look to others for advice. And whether they know it or not, they do, every day, accept the opinions of others and adopt them as their own. Those who boast the loudest of their independence have picked up from someone the idea that independence is a virtue, and their very eagerness to be individualistic is the result of the influence of others. They are what they are because of the counsel they have followed.

"Before we follow any man we should look for the oil on his forehead. We are under no spiritual obligation to aid any man in any activity that has not upon it the marks of the Cross. No appeal to our sympathies, no sad stories, no shocking pictures should move us to put our money and our time into schemes promoted by persons who are too busy to listen to God.

"God has His chosen men still, and they are without exception good listeners. They can hear when the Lord speaks. We may safely listen to such men. But to no others."

Blessed is the man that walketh not in the counsel of the ungodly (Psa. 1:1).

184

Humility "Keeps" the Most

For he is not a Jew, which is one outwardly. . . . But he is a Jew, which is one inwardly . . . whose praise is not of men, but of God (Rom. 2:28, 29).

D. L. Moody could boast of little formal education, and his speech abounded in grammatical errors. His physical appearance was not attractive. His voice was high pitched and his tones nasal. A reporter who was covering his campaigns endeavored to discover the secret of his power. He observed, "I can see nothing whatever in Moody to account for his marvelous work."

Moody chuckled when he heard the comment. "Of course not," he exclaimed. "The work is God's, not mine."

Moody's closest friends knew his secret. Wilbur Chapman said, "I first knew Moody in Louisville, Kentucky, during a campaign he was conducting there. . . .

"After the work had been in progress for some days, and the great Tabernacle on Broadway had been crowded from day to day, and at every meeting, an incident occurred which troubled me greatly, and which I did not fully understand until many months later. At the conclusion of the service a great many workers in the meeting tarried for a moment of conference. A gentleman approached Mr. Moody, 'See this group of ladies on the right of the platform, they are among our prominent women of the City, and support our movement, both with their means and their personal work. They have not yet had the pleasure of shaking hands with you, and they have tarried for this purpose.' 'Where are they?' asked Mr. Moody. The gentleman pointed them out, saying, 'I will tell them you will see them in a few moments.' And in a little while I saw Mr. Moody reach under the pulpit stand for his little felt hat, go out a back door, and taking a cab, drive to his hotel.

"The ladies waited for some time, and finally left with the greatest feeling of indignation, and many of them declaring that they would not again be seen in the meetings and work with a man who could be so rude. I confessed I was puzzled myself, and did not know what explanation could possibly be offered for the strange action.

"Some year or so after this I was in Chicago with him on the platform. Again a woman came to the foot of the stair, and said she wished to see Mr. Moody. 'He was used of God for the salvation of my husband, I want to shake hands with him, and tell him how grateful I feel toward him.'

"I said, 'Why certainly, wait and I will see that you have the privilege of seeing him.' When finally I called his attention to her, and when she had given him her reason for wishing to shake hands with him, without one word he turned and left her. Again, I thought, here is a type of the same thing we saw in Louisville. I comforted the poor woman as best I could.

"A few days later in his conference with young men, he spoke of how we should guard against flattery, and how many strange things we had to do, to prevent the devil from getting a hold upon us. After this conversation I told him of the injustice I had done him in my mind, in the incidents above alluded to. His explanation was very brief but equally satisfactory and to the point. 'If I had shaken hands with those women, I wouldn't have been half through before the devil would have made me believe that I was some great man, and from that time I would have to do as he bid.'

"I was present with him in meetings for a month after this time, and studied him in the light of this explanation, and no one thing has ever helped me more to explain his closeness to God and his humility of Spirit than the facts alluded to."

R. A. Torrey said, "I think D. L. Moody was the humblest man I ever knew in all my life. He loved to quote the words of another: 'Faith gets the most; love works the most; but humility keeps the most.'"

His biographer, W. H. Daniels, said: "Compliments were of no value to him. He regarded them as temptations and snares. He would sometimes say, 'Strike me rather than praise me.' So long as his omnivorous appetite for work was satisfied, nothing else was needed to make him one of the happiest men alive."

The Dwarf Becomes a Giant

Because the foolishness of God is wiser than men; and the weakness of God is stronger than men. . . . But God hath chosen the foolish things of the world to confound the wise; and God hath chosen the weak things of the world to confound the things which are mighty; and base things of the world, and things which are despised, hath God chosen, yea, and things which are not, to bring to nought things that are (1 Cor. 1:25-28).

WE must understand that in Christianity the dwarf is the giant, that the despised, deformed, puny child of faith is, when he recognizes his own weakness and leans upon his own God, big with the force that rolls the stars along. (Dante's idea). —Rendel in *Memoranda Sacra.*

C. T. Studd was one of England's noble and wealthy citizens, but he became poor and was despised on account of the many unconventional methods he pursued. He learned well the secret of true service as the following exhortation reveals: "Whatever you've got, use it for God, and don't wait for what you've not got. If you've only a donkey's jawbone, bray for all you're worth; a braying ass has been known to talk more sense than a Prophet.

"Some 'stuck-up' folks will only blow if they have got silver trumpets. They were rams' horns, not silver trumpets, that blew down the walls of Jericho, not part-songs, but shouts. Silver trumpets are apt to be a great snare to their owners, who waste much time polishing them up, then coddle them in wraps and refuse to use them in God's own open-air cathedrals: not so John Wesley and George Whitefield."

Kings choose their soldiers from the strong and sound
And hurl them forth to battle at command.
Across the centuries, o'er sea and land,
Age after age, the shouts of war resound;
Yet, at the end, the whole wide world around,

Each empty empire, once so proudly planned,
Melts through time's fingers like the dropping sand.

But once a King — despised, forsaken, crowned
Only with thorns — chose in the face of loss
Earth's poor, her weak, her outcast, gave them love,
And sent them forth to conquer in His name
The world that crucified Him, and proclaim
His empire. Lo! pride's vanished thrones above,
Behold, the enduring banner of the Cross.
— *The Burning Bush.*

St. Bernard's hymns and writings still bless and there is a reason for the enduring quality of his works. He reveals the secret in one of his statements: "Ah, Lord, since in Thy hands the most feeble things gain power and strength, and a reed placed within them becomes a scepter, take Thou my heart; it is but a reed, flexible and versatile, turning with every wind; a hollow reed, empty of charity, of devotion, empty of all good. But from the moment it is placed in Thy hands, it will be filled with the strength of Thy divine Spirit, and will become a generous heart, a firm heart, an ardent and fervent heart, ready to surmount all difficulties, and to make all obstacles give way before its indefatigable perseverance."

Richard Baxter said of himself, "I have been a pen in the fingers of God, and who praises the pen?"

That which comes nearest omnipotence is impotence.
— Unknown.

Perfecting God's Strength

And he said unto me, My grace is sufficient for thee: for my strength is made perfect in weakness. Most gladly therefore will I rather glory in my infirmities, that the power of Christ may rest upon me (2 Cor. 12:9).

IN an old magazine, the *Moody Church News,* a certain incident was related in which the narrator was conversing with a dear Christian brother; this friend was being greatly used of God to spread the Gospel through the printed page. In telling of how this "great ministry came to him when he was without any visible resources," he uttered a profound statement well worth remembering: "I learned," said he, "that there was one thing I could give to God that would add to His perfection."

"And what might that be?" inquired his friend. "I have never thought of anything that one could give to God that would be an addition, in any sense or form."

"Why," was the reply, "it was my weakness. His 'strength is made perfect in weakness.'"

"Our weakness," as someone has so aptly put it, "is but the line for the wheels of God's might and strength to run upon."

There have been those saints who have realized this unerring law of the kingdom, and have yielded to God their weakness that His strength might be perfected in their work. Frances Ridley Havergal wrote many books and hymns which are still on the market today because they were God's wisdom to the world. How utterly she depended on Divine inspiration is revealed in the following quotation:

"My experience is that it is nearly always just in proportion to my sense of personal insufficiency in writing anything, that God sends His blessing and power with it; so I don't wonder that your papers are so sweet and helpful! I think He must give us that total dependence on Him for every word, which can only come by feeling one's own helplessness and incapacity, before He can very much use us. And so I think this very sense of not having gifts is the best and most useful gift of them all. It is so much sweeter to have to look up to Him for every word one writes. I often smile when people call me 'gifted,' and think how little they know the real state of the case, which is that I not only feel that I can't, but really can't, write a single verse unless I go to Him for it and get it from Him. You know I only desire His glory and not F.R.H.'s credit; and I greatly shrink from anything of mine being used only as a sort of compliment to me!"

> The poorest of vessels perform His will.
> For His glory, He chooses the meek!
> Other things men despise
> Are the pride of His eyes.
> He brings good out of ill,
> As He perfects His strength through the weak.
> —Unknown.

Charles Cowman, when a missionary in the Far East, learned the same formula for an abiding work. Let us hear what he says: "If any will dare to venture forth on a path of separation, putting himself from all future aid and from all self-originated effort—content to walk with God alone, with no help from any but Him—such will find that all the resources of the Divine Almightiness will be placed at his disposal, and that the resources of Omnipotence must be exhausted before His cause fail for want of help."

Whatever you and I may be privileged to do for Him, let it be too Scriptural in its character and too decided in its results to be mistaken for the works of men. —Anon.

The Lord Be Magnified

Let such as love thy salvation say continually, The LORD be magnified
(Psa. 40: 16 & 70:4).

J. H. Merle D'Aubigne was among the sixteen young students at a seminary in Geneva who were brought to saving truth under the ministry of Robert Haldane. The Lord honored His own Word as Haldane expounded the book of Romans and the Holy Spirit revealed to them the great salvation of their God. Hitherto they had been ignorant of these great truths, and but for Haldane's teaching would have remained in darkness. We quote from D'Aubigne's *History of the Reformation:*

"Man's impotency, God's omnipotence — such were the two truths which Luther sought to restore. It is a poor religion and a poor philosophy that throws man on his natural strength. That so much vaunted strength of his has been tried for ages; yet, while man of himself has been able to make wonderful attainments in what relates to his earthly existence, he has never been able either to dispel the darkness that hides the knowledge of God from his mind, or to change a single leaning of his heart. The highest degree of wisdom ever attained by ambitious minds or by souls burning with the desire of perfection, has been to despair of themselves.

"The doctrine, then, which discovers to us our own powerlessness, while it tells us of a power from God by which we may do all things, is a generous, consolatory, and an absolutely true doctrine; and great was that reformation which reasserted the glory of Heaven upon earth, and which pleads with man for the prerogatives of the mighty God."

Luther, whom God was pleased to use in the Reformation, learned this truth at his conversion. In a letter to an old brother monk of the monastery at Erfurt, George Spenlein, Luther writes: "I could wish to know how it fares with your soul. Is it not tired of its own righteousness? In fine, does it not pant after—does it not place all its trust in the righteousness of Christ? In our days, many are seduced from it by pride; those especially who give their whole endeavors to being righteous. Not understanding the righteousness of God which is freely given to us in Jesus Christ, they would stand before Him on the strength of their deservings. But that cannot be. You, when you were staying with us were in that error, and I, too, was misled by it. I am still struggling against it and have not yet completely triumphed.

"Oh, my dear brother, learn to know Christ and Christ crucified. Learn to sing to Him a new song, to despair of thyself, and to say to Him, Thou, Lord Jesus, Thou art my righteousness, and I, I am Thy sin. Thou hast taken what was mine and Thou hast given me what was Thine. What Thou wast not, that Thou hast become, in order that I may become what I was not! Beware, oh my dear George, of pretending to such a degree of purity as to cease regarding thyself a sinner, for it is only in sinners that Christ dwells. He came down from Heaven, where He dwelt in the righteous, in order that He might dwell also in sinners. Carefully meditate on this love of Christ, and thou shalt then derive from it the sweets of ineffable consolation. Could our works and our afflictions procure us peace of conscience, why should Christ have died? Thou shalt find peace only in Him, by despairing of thyself and thy works, and by learning by what love He opens His arms to receive thee, taking thy sins upon Him and giving thee all His righteousness."

> A mighty fortress is our God,
>   A bulwark never failing;
> Our helper He, amid the flood
>   Of mortal ills prevailing.
> For still our ancient foe
> Doth seek to work us woe;
> His craft and pow'r are great,
> And, armed with cruel hate,
>   On earth is not his equal.
>   — Martin Luther.

The Depth of Descent

Jesus knowing that the Father had given all things into his hands, and that he was come from God, and went to God; He riseth from supper, and laid aside his garment; and took a towel, and girded himself (John 13:3,4).

FEW writers or preachers have shown more inspiration on the subject of Christ's exaltation and humiliation than did Charles Spurgeon. Let us ascend and descend with him in an extract from one of his sermons:

"My brethren, even the acts of our Lord Jesus Christ in His loving condescension we do not fully understand. Ah, think a minute, how can we? Does not our Lord's love always surpass our knowledge, since He Himself is the greatest of all mysteries?

"Do you understand the higher and the lower points of this transaction? You must comprehend them both before you can see what He has done. 'Jesus knowing that the Father had given all things into His hand.' Can you see the glory of this? Jesus our Lord was conscious that His Father had made Him Head over all things to His Church, and that He had laid the government upon His shoulders, and given Him the key of David, that He might open and no man shut, and shut and no man open.

"He knew assuredly that at His girdle swung the keys of Heaven and death and hell, and that having fulfilled the commission of the Eternal God, He was about to return to His throne. Have you grasped the idea? Do you perceive the glory of which Jesus was conscious? If you have done so, then descend by one long sweep—He, this Lord of all, having all things in His hand, takes off His garments, forgoes the common dress of an ordinary man, and places Himself in the undress of a servant, and wears a towel, that He may do service to His own disciples.

"Can you follow Him from such a height to such a depth? A superior in the East never washes an inferior's feet: Christ acts as if He were inferior to His friends, inferior to those poor fishermen, inferior to those foolish scholars who learned so slowly, with whom He had been so long a time and yet they did not know Him, who soon forgot what they knew, and needed line upon line and precept upon precept.

"Having loved them to the end, He stoops to the extreme of stooping, and bows at their feet to cleanse their defilements. Who, I say, can compute the depth of this descent? You cannot know what Christ has done for you, because you cannot conceive how high He is by nature, neither can you guess how low He stooped in His humiliation and death."

Campbell Morgan has also given us a few thoughts worthy of our attention on this amazing subject to which Christ gave such prime importance just a few hours before His departure: "That knotted towel was the badge of slavery; but here is the remarkable fact that the knotted garment was also the insignia of princes, with the very same method of fastening and tying. The difference was in material—for the slave a rough homespun cloth; for princes purple or gold. I think back through the years; and John saw in that girdle not only the badge of slavery, but the girdle of kingship. We do not forget when he was in Patmos, and he had a vision of this Selfsame One in all His glory, in that marvelous description He has given, among other things he wrote, 'girt about at the breast with a golden girdle.' Yes, he saw that in Patmos, and looking back he saw the sackcloth of the slave transmuted into the glory and purple of sovereignty."

O blessed name of SERVANT! comprehending
    Man's highest honor in his humblest name;
For Thou, God's Christ, that office recommending,
    The throne of mighty power didst truly claim;
He who would rise like Thee, like Thee must owe
His glory only to his stooping low.
                                        —Bethune.

194

Divine Humility

If I then, your Lord and Master, have washed your feet; ye also ought to wash one another's feet. For I have given you an example, that ye should do as I have done to you (John 13:14, 15).

H E riseth from supper, and layeth aside His garment; and He took a towel and girded Himself." This is what the Apostle calls taking upon Himself the form of a servant. The charm of the scene is its absolute simplicity. You cannot imagine Christ posturing to the ages. There was no aiming at effect, no thought of the beauty or humility of the act, as there is when the Pope yearly washes the feet of twelve beggars from a golden basin, wiping them with a towel of rarest fabric! Christ did not act thus for show or pretence, but with an absolutely single purpose of fulfilling a needed office. And in this He set forth the spirit of our redemption.

This is the key to the Incarnation. With slight alteration the words will read truly of that supreme act. He rose from the Throne; laid aside the garments of light which He had worn as His vesture; took up the poor towel of humanity, and wrapped it about His glorious Person; poured His own blood into the basin of the Cross; and set Himself to wash away the foul stains of human depravity and guilt.

As pride was the source of human sin, Christ must needs provide an antidote in His absolute humility — a humility which could not grow beneath these skies, but must be brought from the world where the lowliest are the greatest and the most childlike reign as kings.

This is the key to every act of daily cleansing. We have been washed — once definitely and irrevocably, we have been bathed in the crimson tide that flows from Calvary, but we need a daily cleansing. Our feet become soiled with the dust of life's highways; our hands grimy as our linen beneath the rain of filth in a great city; our lips — as the white doorstep of

195

the house—are fouled by the incessant throng of idle, unseemly and fretful words; our hearts cannot keep unsoiled the stainless robes with which we pass from the closet at morning prime. Constantly we need to repair to the Laver to be washed.

But do we always realize how much each act of confession on our part involves from Christ on His? Whatever important work He may at that moment have on hand; whatever directions He may be giving to the loftiest angels for the fulfillment of His purposes; however pressing the concerns of the Church or the Universe upon His broad shoulders— He must needs turn from all these to do a work He will not delegate. Again He stoops from the Throne, and girds Himself with a towel, and, in all lowliness, endeavors to remove from thee and me the stain which His love dare not pass over. He never loses the print of the nails; He never forgets Calvary and the blood; He never spends one hour without stooping to do the most menial work of cleansing filthy souls. And it is because of this humility He sits on the Throne and wields the scepter over hearts and worlds.

This is the key to our ministry to each other. I have often thought that we do not often enough wash one another's feet. We are conscious of the imperfections which mar the characters of those around us. We are content to note, criticize, and learn them. We dare not attempt to remove them. This failure arises partly because we do not love with a love like Christ's—a love which will brave resentment, annoyance, rebuke, in its quest—and partly because we are not willing to stoop low enough. —F. B. Meyer.

> What condescension,
> Bringing us redemption . . .
> God, gracious, tender,
> Laid aside His splendor,
> Stooping to woo, to win, to save my soul.
> —W. E. Booth-Clibborn.

Washing Away the Earth-Touch

If I then, your Lord and Master, have washed your feet, ye also ought to wash one another's feet (John 13:14).

THAT dear Chinese brother in Christ, Watchman Nee, whose books have helped so many, has a slightly different aspect of the same truth which F. B. Meyer so ably expounded in the previous reading. A quotation from one of his books, *Twelve Baskets Full,* gives us much food for thought:

"It will help us to recall that when this incident took place the Jews wore sandals, which gave little protection from the dust of the roads; it was therefore customary after a journey to bathe the feet. But what is stressed here is the positive rather than the negative: renewal rather than removal of defilement. When our Lord washed the disciples' feet He did not censure them for having contracted defilement by the way, nor did He exhort them to walk more carefully. For dust to attach to the feet of the traveler as he walked the dusty roads was inevitable; therefore it was not a rebuke that was called for, but the application of a little water to the soiled and weary feet. In His love the Lord rendered this service to His disciples.

"As long as citizens of Heaven are pilgrims in this world, even while they press on their way in accordance with the purpose of God, they have to tread the earthly roads and their feet are bound to bear traces of earth. . . . Even when we are careful to avoid all that would defile, there are times when, quite unaccountably, we lack zest to press on. The trouble is, the earth-touch has taken toll of us. We have grown footsore with the roughness and dust of the road and this eventually has sapped our strength. We have life; we received that by new birth; but life has lost its freshness and we need renewing.

"It is not the whole body that needs bathing, but the feet need it, and they need it repeatedly, for the end of the road is not reached in a day. . . .

"The washing of feet is not only a service performed by the Lord Himself; it is a ministry committed by Him to the Church. And it is not necessarily a clearly defined institution that is deliberately observed. It is often an unconscious mutual ministration, as when one believer meets another in the Lord and the two converse spontaneously; or when, after a day's work in school or office or factory you are too weary to read the Word or pray, but you attend a weekday church gathering and as you meet some of your fellow-saints you are strangely refreshed. Definably or indefinably, something transpires, and you can go on again with renewed vigor.

"In the intercourse of the saints this feet-washing is of great importance. We are all in frequent need of a ministration of life, and this ought to be mutual: 'Ye also ought to wash one another's feet . . .'

"Once a brother attended the regular meeting for the preaching of the Word. He felt so dull and unresponsive that he wondered if he had sinned against the Lord, but he could get no registration of sin. He tried to discover what had happened to him, but he sought in vain for an explanation. He attempted to throw off the lethargy which seemed to have settled upon him, but it was no good. Presently a brother prayed, and the lethargy was gone. He had been impotent to throw it off, but the freshness of life ministered to him through that brother's prayer instantly dispelled the death that had begun to sap his vitality. . . .

"A certain sister who over the years had learned to draw daily on the life of Christ was always a source of quickening to others. If you felt spiritually jaded, you just needed to call on her and sit down in her company for a little time. You did not need to do anything, nor did she. You simply sat there for a while, and the weariness vanished. You revived because she was in constant close communion with the Lord. . . .

"It is as we abide in freshness of fellowship with Him that we can be freshness of life to those with whom we come in contact. Life is conveyed spontaneously, not by strenuous effort. True, the washing of feet is with water, but we do not need to pump the water up laboriously; it comes to us freely as we live in Him Who is the Water of Life."

Get in Orbit

In him we live, and move, and have our being (Acts 17:28).

MAN got out of orbit when he refused to obey God in the Garden. He has been out of orbit ever since. Ruin and havoc reign as he, out of harmony with God's universe, determines his own circuit. It is only when man comes back to God, confessing that he is hopelessly lost and needing direction, that he is introduced into God's harmonious plan for which he has been created and redeemed.

The soul of every believer is a kingdom where the Redeemer is seen ascending the steps of the palace so long usurped and degraded, penetrating in more or less rapid succession to its chambers, and in due time mounting, in undisputed authority, its throne.

The soul is the chaos of a universe, and the work of Christ is to recreate this shattered and blasted immensity, and compel everything to circulate in harmony around the central sun. He will create in every believer's heart a heaven and to all eternity reign there as sovereign Redeemer. —George Bowen.

Thou hast created me, a universe complete —
So vast when viewed alone, so infinitesimal
When seen amidst the galaxies of globes
Revolving round their sun. And I, sometimes,
I have grown tired of my course,
And wish to choose an orbit of my own,
Veer where I would in space, choose my own speed,
Make my own journey.

Then, when tempted to rebel,
I realize just how much I need my sun. Without Him
Naught would grow; life would become extinct;
All freeze: my glorious ball become a frozen mass.

And yet how slow my course, how modified my pace
Compared to shooting meteors which flash their way along.
Indeed, I notice sometimes, when I faster go,
I feel that this is life indeed!
Then why this forced submission to the sun?
Why need he rule like autocrat supreme?
And so I spin away, try my own course, but no!
I cannot do it, cannot move save in that orbit
Round my sun, for further from his pull, I slow;
My speed declines; I see that energy is but from Him;
If I must move, I must keep near the Source.

O glorious Sun of Righteousness,
In orbit around Thee my world is safe—
Fruit grows, plants flourish, life abounds.
But if You turn Your face, withdraw Your heart,
Your warmth, Your energy one moment, then I cease
To be an entity at all. Spirit of life, of love,
Of everything I need, thank You
For ruling me, rebellious earth.
Now every blade that springs
And every breath records Thy power.
Were I the sun I'd scorch my earth one moment;
Next, I'd freeze its surface or collide;
Catastrophe not order would result if I would rule.
But Thou, how wonderful Thy ways, how perfect
Is Thy plan. How glad I am, dear Lord,
Thou art the Sun and I, a little earth, Thy man.
　　　　　　　　　　　　　　—Trudy Tait.

If there were any smallest star in heaven that had no place
to fill, that oversight would beget a disturbance which no
Leverrier could compute, because it would be a real and eternal, and not merely casual or apparent disorder. . . .

There is, then, I conclude, a definite and proper end,
or issue, for every man's existence; an end, which, to the
heart of God, is the good intended for him, or for which he
was intended; that which he is privileged to become, called
to become, ought to become; that which God will assist
him to become and which he cannot miss, save by his own
fault. —Horace Bushnell.

On Collision Course or in Orbit

My time is not yet come: but your time is alway ready (John 7:6).

"YOUR time is alway ready," said Jesus to His brethren who were pressing Him to go down to Jerusalem for the feast; "My time is not yet come." The Son was in perfect timing with His Father's purposes. "But when the fulness of the time was come, God sent forth his Son" (Gal. 4:4). Though equal with God, it was not for Him to decide His own course. His brethren, however, had not as yet arrived at that point where they had ceased to chart their own course, decide their own time, and walk whither they would.

Elijah has a wonderful history in the Old Testament. When he kept within the orbit of God's will, he was sustained by ravens at the brook Cherith. Then, when directed to go to the widow of Zarephath, he found that the barrel of meal and the cruse of oil never failed all during famine. Later, on Mount Carmel, heavenly fire came down, attesting his sacrifice. But when he fled because of Jezebel's threats, he got out of orbit until a kind Father sent an angel to sustain him for forty days and tell him how to regain course.

Peter, one of God's chosen disciples, had gotten out of orbit when he went back to fishing. Regardless of his previous know-how, he toiled all night and caught nothing. Christ taught him a lesson on how to fish successfully for the souls of men. "At thy command," brought the net full of fish. Then came Peter's call from fishing to shepherding the sheep: "Verily, verily, I say unto thee, When thou wast young, thou girdedst thyself, and walkedst whither thou wouldest: but when thou shalt be old, thou shalt stretch forth thy hands, and another shall gird thee, and carry thee whither thou wouldest not" (John 21: 18).

At Pentecost, those same brethren who had been previously at odds as to who should be the greatest, were all of one accord, for they had gotten into orbit. Directions from an Unseen Guide would henceforth be the determining factor in their work. How remarkable the perfect timing of Ananias when he was sent to Saul praying in Damascus! A prepared teacher met a prepared soul and, as a result, something happened!

Equally remarkable was Philip's leading of the Spirit to leave revival scenes to go "desert way" in order to meet one Ethiopian eunuch. At the exact moment when the eunuch was reading Isaiah, the human instrument sent of God joined the chariot and showed him the way of salvation through Christ. Or consider the timing in Peter's going to the home of the centurion where he and his household were waiting for a message. The hunger of a household was seen by the Divine Father Who sent a teacher to meet their need. Consequently, something supernatural took place! How many of God's ministers today know such timing?

Christ's last prayer in John 17 was for those He was leaving behind. He desired that they be in the same harmonious orbit that He had been in with His Father. "That they all may be one; as thou, Father, art in me, and I in thee, that they also may be one in us; that the world may believe that thou hast sent me." The Father would send the Holy Spirit to guide them into all truth; only such a One Who knew the mind of God so intimately, would be able to detect the timing of the Divine Clock.

Are you on a collision course, choosing your own time and walking "whither thou wouldest," or have you gotten into orbit with God in His spiritual universe? What rest of soul, what harmony, what peace and joy there remains for the individual who, dying to his own preferences, gives over into God's hands the timing, planning, and ambitions of his life! Then, and then only, can he truly discover the truth of Jesus' words: "As the Father hath sent me, so send I you."

—Lillian Harvey.

Nuggets from Ephesians

Volume 1

From the Files of E.F. & L. Harvey

It is with great pleasure that we of Harvey Publishers present this book on the first three chapters of Ephesians. It is a compilation in the truest sense, and cannot be truly called a commentary. It contains only the selections from the files which were the most pithy and full of meat.

Owing to recent illness, Lillian Harvey is no longer able to be personally involved in this venture. Some faithful friends, however, have enabled this book to become a reality, and we are delighted to see one of Lillian's dreams come true. It was her longing, as it is ours, that these files would continue to be used and to bear fruit. *176 pages — $7.50*

Elisha

by Robert Cox

Robert Cox, Welsh evangelist and Bible teacher, was a close friend of the Harveys for many years. From the famous Ascot Race Course in England to the shores of India, the Holy Spirit led this man in the most unusual ways to witness for His precious Lord Jesus Christ. When he hesitatingly showed the manuscript of Elisha to Lillian Harvey, she was convinced that the writings of such an obedient servant of God should be in print.

This book is a series of meditations on the life of Elisha. It is, in essence, a devotional commentary, and brings the reader fresh insight into the life of this remarkable prophet. The Spirit's illumination breathes through each page. We are confident that this book will be a rich blessing as it is the fruit of much meditation and reliance on the Word. *228 pages — $10.00*

Scripture Index

Author Index